Mosquito at War

Mosquito
at War

Chaz Bowyer

LONDON

IAN ALLAN LTD

To the men of the Mosquitos
There be of them, that have left a name behind them,
that their praises might be reported.
And some there be which have no memorial . . .

Ecclesiasticus
Chapter 44, Verse 9

First published 1973
Third impression 1989

ISBN 0 7110 0474 9

Published by Ian Allan Ltd, Shepperton, Surrey; and printed
by Ian Allan Printing Ltd at their works at Coombelands in
Runnymede, England

Contents

Photo Credits

The illustrations in this book were obtained from the following sources:

Associated Press, pages 41 (top right), 56 (bottom left).

British Newspapers Association, pages 95 (bottom left), 99 (bottom), 116 (top), 118 (top).

Canadian Archives, page 57 (top).

Charles E. Brown, pages 41 (centre), 140 (top).

Group Captain H. E. Bufton, page 124 (top left).

Central Press, page 17 (bottom).

Crown Copyright, pages 13 (top), 18 (bottom), 117 (centre), 119 (bottom right), 138 (top left and middle left), 142 (top and centre).

T. Cushing, page 83 (centre).

Flight International, pages 22, 23, 24, 25, 38 (centre), 39 (top right), 40 (top left), 44 (top), 45, 54 (bottom), 55 (top left and top right), 56 (top left and centre), 62 (bottom), 64 (top and bottom left), 94 (centre), 140 (bottom), 143 (bottom).

Fox Photos, page 65 (top).

Hawker-Siddeley Aviation, Hatfield, pages 10, 12 (all), 17 (top), 18 (top), 19 (top and bottom), 29, 40 (middle right and bottom), 41 (bottom), 55 (bottom), 58 (top left and bottom), 77 (top), 84, 89, 90, 95 (centre), 98 (top), 100 (top left, centre and bottom), 111 (inset), 113 (top), 120, 124 (middle left and bottom), 125 (top right), 126 (bottom right), 135, 136, 139 (top and bottom left).

S. Howe, pages 83 (bottom), 140 (centre).

Illustrated Magazine, pages 38 (top), 54 (top left), 61 (inset), 82.

Imperial War Museum, pages 7, 30, 31, 34, 35, 38 (bottom left), 39 (bottom left), 54 (middle left), 58 (top right), 59 (all), 79, 80 (bottom left), 83 (top), 88 (top), 95 (bottom right), 96 (bottom), 97 (bottom left and right), 99 (top right and middle right), 101 (middle right), 108 (middle and bottom), 109 (middle and bottom), 113 (bottom), 117 (bottom right), 124 (centre right), 126 (bottom left), 127 (top), 131, 132, 133, 144.

Keystone Press Agency, Frontispiece and pages 39 (bottom right), 40 (middle left), 41 (top left), 62 (left), 65 (bottom), 94 (top), 101 (top), 109 (top), 112 (top).

Flight Lieutenant J. A. R. Leask, page 96 (middle left).

Squadron Leader Howard Lees, pages 122 (top and centre), 123 (top and middle left).

New York Times, pages 78, 108 (top).

Planet News Agency, page 81 (bottom).

Royal Australian Air Force PRO, pages 57 (bottom left), 58 (centre), 141 (centre).

Royal Canadian Air Force, pages 125 (bottom right), 126 (top left).

Radio Times Hulton Picture Library, pages 118 (bottom right), 119 (centre).

Wing Commander F. Ruskell, pages 77 (bottom), 124 (top right).

L. Southern, page 116 (middle left).

J. W. R. Taylor, page 143 (top right).

G. T. Thomas, page 118 (bottom left).

Topix Agency, pages 63 (bottom), 95 (top right), 107 (inset), 127 (bottom right), 142 (bottom).

The remainder are from the Author's collection.

Foreword
by Sir Max Aitken
Bart, DSO DFC,

Strike Wing boss. Group Captain Max Aitken DSO DFC who led the multi-squadron Banff Wing of Coastal Command.

By the end of the war the Mosquito was, if not the most famous aircraft of the RAF—the Spitfire was probably that—the most popular with the men who flew aeroplanes. It had many virtues and many uses from bombing to photographic reconnaissance. It was an enormously *successful* aircraft. Since then its fame has grown.

Yet its origin was almost accidental. When the war began it was obvious that a great amount of material and manpower in the furniture-making industry was not going to be needed. Was it to be allowed to go to waste? Somebody then had the notion of making a *wooden* aeroplane.

That seemed a revolutionary idea in those days; it seems pretty audacious even now. But the project was blessed; the aeroplane was designed and built and from the very beginning aroused the enthusiasm of everyone who flew her or saw her. The Mosquito was a sensation.

In this book of Chaz Bowyer's is to be found a collection of the experiences of men who flew Mosquitos. They are extraordinarily vivid, authentic and convincing. This is the war as it was lived by men of the RAF flying one particular type of aircraft. But what emerges at the end is something more than a series of human adventures.

It is the personality of an aircraft which aroused the affection of hundreds of men who flew in her during desperate days.

Read and I think you will see why.

Introduction

Mosquito—'Mossie'—probably the most evocative name of World War II for a generation of air and ground crews of the Royal Air Force. Its fame was world-wide, its achievements have become legendary. From a purely economic viewpoint, the de Havilland 98 Mosquito was undoubtedly one of the most adaptable, efficient and versatile aircraft of its era. It could carry a staggering variety of hardware, yet retained the performance of a fighter, the fluid manoeuvrability of an aerobat, the ruggedness of a battle cruiser and an ability to 'bring 'em back alive' that endeared it to its 'drivers' and 'conductors'.

It is rare for any aeroplane on being introduced to the RAF to escape condemnation from some quarter—yet the Mossie was one. Almost without exception, crews always praised the Mosquito, whatever its particular role. Only in Burma were there any cryptic comments about the 'Termite's Dream'—and such criticism was confined to the early arrivals in that operational theatre before experience modified certain technical aspects and solved its Far East problems.

The factual history of the Mosquito has been told in many forms, especially noteworthy being the admirable tome, *Mosquito*, by M. C. Sharp and M. J. F. Bowyer (no relation). In this book an attempt has been made to show at least some of the multitudinous facets of the Mossie and the men associated with it during the period 1939-45 only; but it should be borne in mind that the Mosquito continued to give frontline service with the RAF for many years of the so-called 'peace', the last official Mosquito operational sortie being flown on December 15th, 1955 by Mosquito PR34A, RG314, of 81 Squadron, Seletar, Singapore. To have tried to cover every possible aspect of the myriad operational uses of the Mosquito would probably require ten more volumes —and even then only a rubbing of the full story's surface could have been obtained. So this book is merely a sampling, a tentative dip into the seemingly bottomless pool of Mosquito lore.

Like the Spitfire, Hurricane and Lancaster, the Mosquito has come to be virtually identified with a host of well-known individual pilots; men like Leonard Cheshire VC, Bob Bateson, Peter Wykeham, Basil Embry, Bob Braham and a hundred others who added lustre to the aircraft's impressive record of war service. But it should never be forgotten that it was the lesser-known and unpublicised crews who made up the vast bulk of the aircraft's splendid operational effort. The men named (rightly in my view) have received a measure of well-deserved fame for their exploits. I am certain that they would be the first to agree that it was to the ordinary crews that the majority of successes should be attributed. Therefore, the real spine of the narrative herein is comprised of personal accounts by the silent majority.

Most of these accounts were generously contributed after no little persuasion, due to the constant horror of any fighting Serviceman of being accused of the deadliest sin—'line-shooting', by a tiny selection of the many hundreds of men who flew Mosquitos to war. To them, my gratitude for allowing me to pull away the discreet bushes they have been hiding behind for too long. Much of the remaining narrative is a personal selection from various accounts and records. While I have deliberately tried to avoid the well-publicised histories of individual exploits, there is one notable exception—the last sortie of Group Captain P. C. Pickard DSO DFC and his inseparable companion, Flight Lieutenant J. A. Broadley DSO DFC DFM. It is merely my opinion, but I have always regarded these men and that operation as probably the finest examples of courage, devotion to duty and sheer professional skill during the 1939-45 war in the air. Others may have equalled that peak—none surpass it.

Of the many photographs used in illustration in this book, a number have appeared in the past in other contexts. The fact that a photograph has been published elsewhere is not (in my view) any good reason for automatically discarding it in a new book. Nevertheless, I have tried to provide the reader with as many 'new' photographs as possible within the context of the subject matter, my criterion overall being simply a desire to offer the best available picture value. I have deliberately excluded many possible illustrations depicting Mosquitos and their crews which 'failed to return'— having absolutely no wish to cause grief or suffering to surviving relatives and friends of the men depicted. Of enormous help in tracking down particular photographs for this book, and providing invaluable assistance in this direction, were many good friends and acquaintances. Phil Birtles and Ted Hunt of Hawker-Siddeley offered their usual unstinted help, Bruce Robertson came to my assistance for the umpteenth time, Ann Tilbury of *Flight International* gave me virtually carte blanche in her unsurpassed photo files. Ted Hine of the Imperial War Museum put himself out to the greatest degree to help, despite difficult circumstances at the time. Equally generous with their help and advice were Chris Ashworth, Phil Jarrett, J. Richard Smith, Paul Sampson, Tommy Cushing, Stuart Howe, John Taylor, Chris Shores, Geoff Thomas, Rex King, Howard Lees, Alan Stephens—to each of them my grateful thanks. I am indebted to Miss Amy Howlett of William Kimber for permission to reproduce an extract from *Duel Under the Stars* by Wilhelm Johnen; as I am to the late Flight Lieutenant B. S. Northway for an extract from his history of 107 Squadron, RAF.

Finally a word of thanks to my publishers for their patience in bearing with the several delays and minor tribulations I caused during compilation, and their apparent confidence in my ability to produce the book. In this context I am especially indebted to Geoffrey Freeman Allen and the man who 'started it all', John W. R. Taylor.

This then was the Mosquito and these were the types of men who flew or 'mothered' this superb aeroplane. Perhaps those men will accept my book as it is intended—one man's tribute to them all.

Norwich, 1973.   CHAZ BOWYER

Out of the Chrysalis

Left: The 'yellow bird' is unwrapped. The first Mosquito, serialled EO234 originally, at Hatfield on November 19th, 1940, being prepared for its maiden flight a few days later. Painted yellow overall for easy identification by defence guns and aircraft, its colour somehow emphasised the sleek contours.

Middle left: Roll-out. EO234 is eased out of the Hatfield Flight Test hangar on November 21st, 1940—an anxious moment for the de Havilland team. There were then only four days to go before the result of their hopes and labours was to receive its baptism of the air. Meanwhile engine runs, fuel checks, hydraulic tests and a hundred other sundry, but vital items had to be done.

Bottom left: On to the grass for an engine run and fuel consumption check. EO234 in the pale winter sunshine of November 1940 on a final run-through before being trusted to the elements.

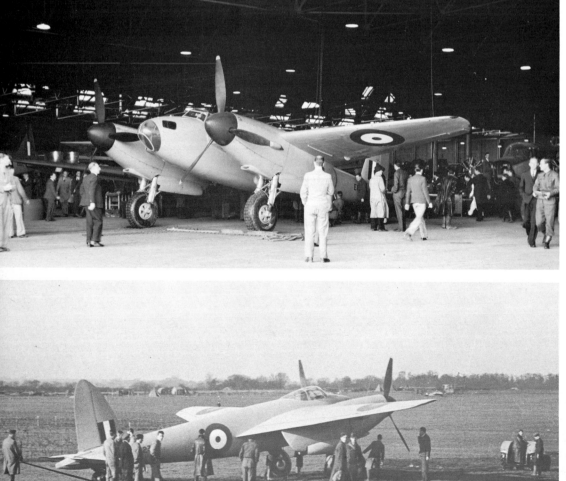

Right: Ready to go—the quiet moment before the first air test. Still bearing the works serial EO234, the first-ever Mosquito awaits its destiny. The dark appearance of the yellow paint-finish here was due to the use of ortho film but unwittingly previsaged the later soot-black night fighter versions. In the background, a Westland Lysander.

Right: Test flight, January 10th, 1941. Now re-serialled as W4050, the first Mosquito had completed 30 air check flights by December 11th, 1940 and marked up her century on April 14th, 1941.

Below: Yet another landing is recorded in the extensive test programme of W4050. A perfect touch-down which also displays the compact simplicity of line of the design.

Development

Top: High Flyer. The prototype photo-reconnaissance Mosquito, W4051, is prepared for flight-testing at Hatfield on June 12th, 1941. With its proven speed and altitude performance, the employment of the Mossie in PR work was given priority.

Above: Run-up. The trolley accumulator is disconnected as W4051 is given a final ground-run and wheel-brake test prior to taxying out for a pre-delivery check flight, June 12, 1941.

Right: The variety expands, W4057, prototype B MkV, remains earthbound while another significant 'sister', W4052, first of the deadly Mosquito fighters, shows its paces overhead, Hatfield, September 5th, 1941. The yellow P marking stood for prototype—a standard livery for the precious 'first' versions of all Service aircraft of the period.

Left: DZ313, a typical BIV light bomber version on a local flight over the Hertfordshire countryside in 1942. The basic outline of the Mosquito was little altered throughout the war despite the myriad additions and installations necessitated by the ever-changing needs of operations. The two-piece front windscreen is evident, but was soon replaced by a bullet-proof alternative in view of the hazard of bird-strikes encountered during low-level bombing operations.

Below: Another BIV bomber is rolled out for initial flight checks and eventual collection by the Air Transport Auxiliary crews for delivery to an operational unit. By December 1942, 415 Mosquitoes had been produced, half of these being then in front-line service; and by the end of the war a total of 6,710 had been built—nearly 50 per cent by the parent de Havilland company, supported superbly by over 400 sub-contractors

Right: Filming history—Geoffrey de Havilland prepares to take up a Mosquito fighter on June 2nd, 1944 as part of a film reconstruction of the Mosquito's historic first-flight from Salisbury Hall—in fact the scene here is at Hatfield. In the fighter version it was necessary to relocate the bottom entrance, hatch door of the original design to provide for a side entry door.

Middle right: Close companion—a fighter in day camouflage noses close for the benefit of the camera, its four .303 Browning machine guns providing a deadly row of "teeth" and backed by the even deadlier four 20mm cannons in the belly. In fighter Mosquitos a flat-fronted, one-piece windscreen, proof against bullets or birds, replaced the angled two-piece bomber windscreen.

Below: 'Cat's Eyes'—the radar-equipped night fighter displaying its nose radar barb and wing-tip AI aerials which provided the crew with an ability to pierce the blackness of night. DD609, an NF Mk II in March 1942, prior to delivery to 151 Squadron where Flight Lieutenant Moody and Flying Officer Marsh claimed a Dornier 217 E-4 bomber on the night of June 26th, 1942 in this aircraft. The lamp-black finish, supposedly non-reflecting, was later discarded for night fighters.

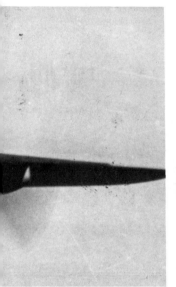

Top right: Hatfield scene on February 12th, 1942. Night fighter Mk IIs, W4090, W4092 and W4088 patiently awaiting their pilots from ATA to ferry them to the operational scene. On July 21st, 1942, W4090, piloted by Pilot Officer Fisher of 151 Squadron destroyed a Dornier 217 E-4 over the North Sea and . . .

. . . right: the men who were about to ferry them. Second pilot from right is the internationally famous Jim Mollison, pre-1939 record-breaker and racing pilot. Early in the war, a group of women ATA pilots, under the command of Miss Pauline Gower, made Hatfield their base for Mosquito ferrying to the first operational squadrons.

Oboe Navigator
Frank Ruskell

What did it feel like to climb into a Mosquito and fly to war? In the course of many interviews and a minor mountain of correspondence with ex-Mosquito men, one point was always emphasised—the sheer beauty of the aircraft. Its aesthetically pleasing shape bred a form of love affaire between man and machine, an affinity which brought with it a feeling of confidence that the aeroplane would never let you down. To men who literally faced death on every sortie, such a oneness with their aircraft meant one less hazard to face, a comforting feeling of safe refuge from anything that the enemy or pure fate could throw against them. Frank Ruskell was one such man who became enraptured with the design. Flying in the righthand seat, he soon came to fully appreciate the sheer quality of the Mosquito. As a member of the pioneer *Oboe* squadron, 109, his tasks were exacting, demanding

First operational squadron of Mosquito bombers was No 105, stationed at Marham, Norfolk, which received its first BIV bomber on April 11th, 1942—though its crews had been training with earlier versions since November, 1941 when Geoffrey de Havilland brought W4064 to Swanton Morley, 105's base in that month. It fell to 105 Squadron to test the principle theory behind construction of the Mosquito that sheer speed and no armament (for defence) would provide complete safety on war sorties. Here, DZ367, (J) receives its complement of four 500lb medium capacity (MC) high explosive (HE) bombs on December 24th, 1942 at Marham, Norfolk. The squadron's first operations with Mossies were flown on the morning of May 31st, 1942 as a 'tail-end' follow-up to the previous night's first 1,000-bomber raid on Cologne by a Bomber Command main force.

the very best from crew and aircraft. Neither failed.

The first thing that struck one about the Mosquito was the beauty of line of the fuselage, tailplane, fin and engine cowlings. They all went together and made a lovely aeroplane. The cockpit cover also had a sweet line and the simplicity of the undercarriage and the treaded tyres set the whole thing off. The aeroplane sat on the ground looking pert and eager and it was easy to become fond of—which was by no means true of all aeroplanes, the Hampden for example. These were my feelings about the BIV. The line was marred in the MkVI by the flat windscreen and the protruding guns. When the BIX came along, it looked even better than the BIV because the engines were larger and the spinners extended forward of the line of the nose (the later Hornet had a similar feature). This gave the line added beauty and also conveyed an air of warlike viciousness which was very apt.

Inside the cockpit there was just room for the crew to do what they had to do. The pilot sat in the usual sort of seat, with his seat pack and dinghy; the navigator sat on the main spar on his dinghy, but with his parachute pack elsewhere for lack of headroom. In the *Oboe* version the nose

was full of black boxes and the *Gee* and bomb switches were near his left elbow. used to push my parachute pack on top o the boxes in the nose, out of the way—yo could not leave it on the floor as that wa the escape hatch. The navigator in th *Oboe* version had a little navigatio board, made on the squadron, on which was screwed the two parts of a Dalto computer-triangle and Appleyard scale— and on which you pinned your chart There was also a little box let into the to where you kept the protractor, pencils etc The plotting chart we used was a 1 million *Gee* chart. Our routes to and from the English coast were fixed, and ou range was such that you never went of the printed *Gee* chart.

Oboe attacks were always started from 'waiting point', ten minutes' flying tim from the target. Up to that point yo followed a Bailey Beam for track accuracy monitoring on *Gee* (once or twice th beams were laid wrong . . .) and checkin the ground speed between *Gee* fixes Operating in this rigid pattern, we wer able to ensure navigation and timing accuracy of a high order—the recor speaks for itself . . . For greater range o the *Oboe*, we flew as high as the aircraf would go—which meant climbing o track with consequent complications to th

down. On a *Musical Parramatta* everybody *knew* that the red TIs would be spot-on.

We were also very proud of our timing accuracy, but there were times when individual aircraft failed to drop their markers due to enemy interference with the *Oboe* signals. These occasions caused us some distress as we knew the 'heavies' down below were taking a pasting on their run-in, expecting the TIs to go off in front of them. Of course, when all went well we had a most marvellous grandstand view of a technical triumph. The first *Oboe* aircraft in could be heard by the others and they knew when to watch for the TIs bursting. Before that you could follow his progress down the run by the concentration of flak and searchlights, because 'Jerry' knew what was coming. Lower down, the 'heavies' would be battling through, and only a couple of minutes after the first TI, the bombs would begin to go off—HE and incendiaries right on the TIs. The back-up

navigation. We were, however, able to reach operating height before we ran out of *Gee* cover, so we were able to maintain accuracy. As we experienced wind shear in the climb, the pilot could detect it by the change in heading (or 'course' as it was known then) to maintain constant direction on the Bailey Beam. Coming back to England from the Ruhr area, we used to do a cruise descent which brought us home at a tremendous speed (for those days). We always went out at Southwold and came in at Orfordness, so that the little tracks from your base to these points used to get smudged with rubbing-out *Gee* fixes all the time.

Pathfinder operations were of two kinds —Sky-marking, code-named *Wanganui;* and ground-marking, known as *Parramatta*. If the primary marking was to be done by the *Oboe* Mosquitos, the operations were known as *Musical Wanganui* or *Musical Parramatta*. Because of the characteristics of *Oboe*, the 'musical' operations gave marking accuracy of the highest order (100-200 yards error) and were welcomed by everybody involved. For technical reasons *Oboe* could only put markers down every five minutes (in the earlier and busier days, anyway), so certain of the 'heavy' Pathfinders used to keep our markers stoked up until the next lot came

Ready to go—a 105 Squadron line-up with all engines running and about to taxy away, Marham, December 1942. Reading from front are DZ360 (A), DZ353 (E), DZ367 (J), DK338 (P), DZ378 (K) and DZ379 (H).

green TIs would keep coming down and every five minutes new *Oboe* reds—spot-on the target as everybody watching knew. As you pulled away for home you could see the whole thing—TIs, bombs, incendiaries flak searchlights, aircraft in flames, fighter fire—and of course the fires on the ground. On a good clear night, I used to be able to read my wristwatch in the fires—and that is the truth! We used to screech home like bullets and the crew could be back in the Mess quite early.

When there was no marking for us to do, we used to go on nuisance raids into the Ruhr and Rhineland, taking off at half-hour intervals from about half an hour before sunset, with a load of four or six 500lb HE bombs. We used to go to different targets all over the Ruhr and Rhineland areas and it was quite possible to see chaps on other targets being pasted by flak—black aircraft in searchlights look silver, anyway. These sorties were rather different from the true marker sorties, as you were on your own and the Jerries knew what you were up to. There was the odd night when nobody fired at you, but they were few and far between. We were laid on pinpoint targets, needless to say. If you were on one of these trips, you might take off just after four on a winter's afternoon, fly the trip, go through interrogation and be back in the Mess before 8 pm. I remember once going into the Mess ante-room in battle dress at about that time and the Padre ('Bish' Bradford)

said, 'Are you on tonight, Junior?', and I said 'I've been'. It was quite uncanny.

We were occupied like this during the winter of 1943-44 when the 'heavies' went further afield and PFF was using H2S. Before and after D-Day, we used the *Oboe* accuracy to go for flying-bomb (V1) sites in northern France. Each site would have a couple of *Oboe* Mosquitos to mark it and 20-30 'heavies' to bomb it. When we were on a target in the Pas de Calais, we used to start our *Oboe* runs over the Thames Estuary—quite a change! But we hardly regarded these as 'operations'. I left the squadron in April 1944 and did not take part in D-Day or post-D-Day operations.

What was it like? There was a feeling of relative immunity given by height and speed. There was also the feeling of great responsibility when you were dropping primary markers. If you were the first aircraft of all, the worry was immense—quite apart from the fact that you knew you were going to get the undivided attention of the defences. One sat up there in the dark with a grandstand or bird's eye view and could see the muzzle flashes of the guns as they opened up at you. You knew you had to wait half a minute or so for the shells to climb up to where you were, and all this time the guns kept going off and you knew the shells were climbing up. Mercifully, they mostly went off behind and below, but not always. You sat in your little wooden aeroplane, hanging on to its props, watching the show, with the *Oboe*

signals coming in and everything else silence. The navigator used to have his head-set wired so that he had the pilot's signal (the *Cat*) in one ear and his own (the *Mouse*) in the other. I used to sit on the floor to tune the gear and trim the aerial. Then, when I was satisfied, at say five minutes to target, I used to sit up on my seat again and watch the fireworks. Often you could smell the flak and, on alarming occasions, hear it. The searchlights were blinding and pilots used to drop their seats so that they could see the instruments better. I have sometimes been looking at a bit of sky where a shell went off and seen the red-hot bits of metal fly out— this is no exaggeration. The aircraft used to get peppered quite often and I had two bits of flak I picked out of ours one night, which I carried around in my pocket. (I lost them in a pub in Cambridge—and never even knew which pub . . .).

Sometimes the aircraft got knocked off their run at a crucial point by flak bursting under the wings. Of course, you had to recover and press on. Even so, for all the attention we got, you knew it was nothing like what the 'heavies' were getting down below. In the spring and summer of 1943 when the *Oboe*-led offensive on the Ruhr and Rhineland was at its height, the intensity of effort was enormous and I believe crews did whole tours, or nearly so, on these raids.

I said the aircraft used to hang on their props. This was true of the MkIV, but not the MkIX. In the IV the nose was up at a noticeable angle and the coolant vents in the tops of the engine cowlings used to give off vapour at height—you could see it in the moonlight or searchlights and there would be paler streaks across the wings. The IVs battled gallantly on, but the IXs took it in their stride. They had Merlins with two-stage, two-speed superchargers and climbed like the proverbial home-sick angels. We had much more freedom of manoeuvre in IXs and it was a pity we didn't have them for the main offensive. Another feature of the IV was that there was no pressurisation, so that you had difficulty in finding enough breath to speak with. Not knowing any better, we took this in our stride and had a pleasant surprise when we found the MkIX was pressurised.

Early in 1943 when we first flew at 29,000 feet over NW Europe, we occasionally had a rough ride for no apparent reason. You would be flying along towards the target and run into high frequency turbulence. It was like going over a cobbled road on a bicycle with no tyres, and was most alarming as there was no apparent cause. We used to fly out of it in the end but as far as I recall we were never given an explanation. I know now that we were near the tropopause and were in clear-air turbulence caused by a jet-stream. At that time I doubt if the Met-men had formed any clear ideas on jet-streams and it's possible that we were among the first airmen to experience the phenomenon.

We occasionally experienced very strong winds at lower altitudes and I remember once having a drift of 40 degrees. I stuck to my DR and found these winds, but I remember that one crew decided that their compass was u/s and went back to base. We were not really breaking new ground with these experiences because the PR Spitfires and Mosquitos must have had it all before us, but we did not know. The Mosquito was a good-looking aeroplane of very high performance. It seldom let you down and for the *Oboe* role it proved the ideal—there was no other aeroplane at our disposal which could have filled the bill. You could not help loving it and went to war in it with very confidence.

Taxying now—A-Able and E-Easy follow the remainder to the start-point.

From Both Seats
Syd Clayton

Syd Clayton is almost unique in the Mosquito story. Originally an observer in Blenheims with 105 Squadron in 1941, he flew 72 operational sorties before being 'rested' as an instructor. When he heard that his old unit was to be re-equipped with Mosquitos he promptly pulled strings to get back on operations and eventually, flying mostly with Roy Ralston, his erstwhile pilot of Blenheim days, Syd completed a further 28 operations to make his 'century'. He then 'deserted' the Navigators' Union by taking pilot training and, in 1944, returned yet again to the operational scene as a pilot with 464 Squadron RAAF, flying another 45 operations before hostilities ceased in Europe. 105 Squadron had been the first operational Mosquito squadron (though not the first unit) and therefore Syd Clayton's story virtually spans the gamut of Mosquito bomber operations from 1942 to 1945.

It was around February-March 1942, whilst instructing at 17 OTU, Upwood that I heard a whisper that 105 Squadron were re-forming at Swanton Morley with Mossies. I did the necessary spade-work and was posted on June 1st, 1942, when I met the CO, Wing Commander Peter Simmons. We had our first flight as a crew on June 8 in W4065—a cross-country of two hours twenty minutes. The training programme continued but due to a shortage of Mosquitos, we used Blenheims, Bisleys, Oxfords and Master Is because observers had to have W/T training.

I flew my first Mossie op on July 11th, by which time 105 was at Horsham St Faith, Norwich. The aircraft was Mosquito BIV, DK300, our load 4 x 500lb GPs and the target the submarine base at Flensburg. It was a low-level attack and we met medium flak which damaged our fin and rudder, severed the pipe to the pitot head and further damaged the hydraulic system. We had no trouble getting home but due to the damaged hydraulics, the pilot couldn't drop the wheels or lower flaps. Our air speed indicator was u/s and we had to be led in by another aircraft for a belly landing at around 160mph—which, thankfully, was safely accomplished.

From then on we alternated on high and low-level work. Intelligence did a marvellous job in locating flak batteries, particularly along the coast, and consequently a good land-fall was essential on low-level ops. By using the MkIX bomb sight to check drift and the wind direction off the sea lanes, this was accomplished without trouble. Sea gulls were a hazard when crossing over the coast and in the early days (before the thick, bullet-proof windscreens were installed) one or two Mossies had windscreens completely shattered.

A variety of ops were flown in July-September and on October 21st, my 85th op, we were given a roving commission. Our Mosquito was DZ343 and the general idea was to bomb four separate targets in different areas so that, apart from bomb damage. production was lost due to the alerts. We made a general nuisance of ourselves for about three hours and then, crossing the north Dutch coast, we were jumped by two Focke-Wulf 190s who had obviously been vectored on to us. Cloud was about six-tenths at 3-4,000 feet and on sighting the EA, we entered cloud, turned north and dived for the deck. On breaking cloud cover we had gained some distance, but the 190s were being controlled and soon turned on to us. However with our dive we managed to hold them off, although they chased us for about 15 minutes. The big snag was trying to keep a sight on their position and distance away.

The Mossie wasn't fitted with VHF, but we had the Marconi 1154-1155 W/T and the only way one could keep check was to slip your head sideways between the top of the radio and the canopy. Being more or less at sea level and going flat out, it was a very bumpy ride and my head vibrated between radio and canopy. Luckily the Focke-Wulfs finally broke away and we made for base.

Syd Clayton flew a further 14 ops against a wide range of factory and rail targets during November 1942 to March 1943, including another high speed belly landing at base due to flak damage; and his 99th operation was against the Renault Aero works at Le Mans on March 9th. Came April 1st, 1943 (the RAF's 25th 'birthday') and the magic 100th . . .

We went down to the ops room as usual that morning. It was April 1st and the RAF had a birthday. We didn't know yet where or how we were going to celebrate. Noisily, most probably. Over Germany for preference. To me it was more than a

birthday celebration. My eagerness was personal, for I had done 99 trips. For three weeks now I had waited for the century. I wanted it to be something to remember. It was that, all right.

It was 09.30 hours and our Group Captain was in deep consultation with Group Met. It all depended on the weather, as it always did. And the weather was going to be just right. The Group Captain laid on a trip to Trier. The weather experts forecast low cloud and rain extending right across our target area between 1500 hours and 1700 hours. So we would drop in at 1600 hours.

We were to cross the French coast south of Bologne and after that fly practically due east. The front of bad weather would give us cover all the way to our target, some engine repair sheds on the west side of Triers. When all the intricacies of the operation—which included met, routing, intelligence, bomb load and type, cameras and number of aircraft and crews available—had been dealt with, the crews who were to go on the show were called down for briefing. I was getting my

hundredth trip! As navigator in DZ462 to the leading pilot, Roy Ralston. Take-off was to be at 1400 hours, so we lunched in the briefing room. Then, after emptying our pockets, we collected our flying kit, parachutes, Mae Wests, dinghies and emergency rations. The first part of our journey to Trier began—out to the dispersed Mosquitos.

At 1410 hours we were airborne, circling the airfield, waiting for the formations to take position behind us. At 1430 hours we set course and flew down to Beachy Head at between 50 and 100 feet. Down there close to the deck, the sensation of speed was exhilarating. Occasionally a flock of white birds would come hurtling towards us and, at the last moment, flash away to one side or above us. The weather was good. Too good. Cloud base was about 3,000 feet and visibility was good too. We changed course at Beachy Head. The cloud was still high above us and visibility stayed the way it was. We'd had our orders to turn back if we didn't meet with the right kind of cloud cover and it began to look as if this

En route—E-Easy DZ353 of 105 Squadron over an English patchwork countryside carpet heads for Germany. This was a Mosquito frequently flown by Wing Commander Roy Ralston DSO AFC DFM and his inseparable navigator, Flight Lieutenant Syd Clayton DSO DFC DFM.

Low-level. Mosquito bombs bursting among the Le Mans railway yards on March 4th, 1943. Direct hits can be seen on a coaling tower just south-west of the reception sidings and on workshops between the roundhouses. This raid was led by Squadron Leader R. W. Reynolds DSO DFC of 139 Squadron, the second unit to be equipped with bomber Mosquitos.

Top right: Another anti-railway low-level strike by 105 Squadron—this time the St Joseph locomotive works at Nantes on March 23rd, 1943. Eleven Mosquitos made this attack from between 50 and 1,200 feet—and no bomb landed outside the specific target area. The hazard of flying through the smoke from the leading aircraft's bombs at such heights is vividly demonstrated here.

Bottom right: Birthday treat —a surprise 'gift' for the marshalling yards at Ehrang by low-levellers of 105 Squadron on April 1st, 1943, the 25th anniversary of the original formation of the RAF. It was also the occasion of Syd Clayton's 100th operation as a navigator, after which he left 105 for pilot training. His pilot, Roy Ralston, received a DSO after this his 83rd operation.

birthday party was off. Roy decided to carry on a little longer—to within 10 miles of France, anyway. Then, just as I was getting ready to be disappointed, the bad weather the Met men had promised came on to the horizon. Cloud lowered and visibility decreased. We crossed the enemy coast in pouring rain with high spirits and visibility clamped down to 400 yards. It was like this for 230 miles, with cloud covering hills and visibility down to 200 yards or less in places. Nevertheless, the pilots kept good formation.

All this time my job was with my maps and maybe I was a bit more tense than usual. Not only was this my 100th trip, but it was the last operation for Roy and I as a crew. I kept praying I wouldn't get off course or endanger the success of the trip. We skimmed over several aerodromes on the way—just a fleeting glimpse of them and they were gone. Little French villages deserted and fields empty of peasants. The rain, our ally, had driven them all indoors.

France slid swiftly beneath our wings; railways, roads, rivers—all pinpoints on which we had to depend to read our way to Trier. The idea of fighter opposition wasn't bothering me for we had the weather on our side, but the clouds giving

us protection might also be down on the hills around Trier and might prevent us locating and attacking the target. Ten miles west of Luxembourg, however, the weather cleared. Cloud rose to 2,500 to 3,000 feet and visibility lengthened to about ten miles. For a few moments I had a spot of 'finger' trouble. Looking for parallel railway lines, I could only see one line and it wasn't until I looked at my map for a second time that I realised this 'line' was the Luxembourg border! South of Luxembourg, over the German frontier and then on to final course for the target— with an inevitable feeling of excitement beginning to possess me.

Then I saw the smoke from Trier rising above the hills and I suddenly realised that everything was going to be all right. We opened the bomb doors. In a matter of seconds we had nipped over the hills and were roaring down the valley, heading for the target. The photographs we had studied made target location easy enough. Nearer and nearer, expecting a hail of flak at any moment, we raced on. There was the target, dead ahead. I watched Roy's thumb on the bomb button as the sheds came steadily towards us. He sat dead still—and then suddenly his thumb jerked just once, and he laughed.

Then we were away, up the hillside north-east of the town. Looking back, I could see tall columns of black and white smoke rising from the centre of the target. It had been decided that we should follow the bad weather front out over enemy territory and this sheltered us to within 50 miles of the enemy coastline. There the low cloud broke up and we found ourselves with a canopy of cloud about 4,000 feet above us and good visibility. We decided to go up and as we climbed, I looked back and saw the other Mossies coming up with us, still in perfect formation. This was where we expected trouble and some flak did come up from Merville aerodrome, but it did no damage and we were soon comfortably in cloud.

When we came down through it and set final course for home, the enemy coast was far behind us and I looked down and out to the quilt of English fields ahead of us. It was over. I'd done my 100th operational sortie, but I'd also done my last trip with my pilot, Roy Ralston. In a few weeks I'd be flying again, but in a Tiger Moth for I should be beginning my training as a pilot.

After training, Syd Clayton joined 464 Squadron RAAF, a Mosquito unit of 140 Wing, 2nd TAF at Thorney Island and flew the first of 45 more operations in Mossies on August 26th, 1944—a night sortie against rail and road transport, and summarised these by saying 'Nothing terribly exciting happened in my ops as a pilot, apart from odd bits of flak and an occasional brief encounter with night fighters. From a navigator's point of view, I found the Mossie very good. With the introduction of VHF and then *Gee*, plus adequate pre-flight planning, it was a doddle. With two average-sized blokes the cockpit was comfortable and practically side-by-side seating ensured that the Nav could grab the control column if necessary. Maybe the difficulty of baling-out in a rather confined space under any attitude would be a snag, but as I personally never had to, I can't comment. I'm obviously biased regarding the Mossie, but as a pilot I found her a wonderful aircraft which would take a severe hammering and still fly on one engine.'

First Mossie Op

Dick Strachan

On October 1st, 1943 I crewed up with a flying officer pilot for a second tour of operations, having completed one tour on Stirlings. My new pilot was, at the age of 19, one of the youngest pilots ever to complete a tour on Hampdens, but wore the ribbon of a Distinguished Flying Medal. Casting my mind back, I can recall the early months of 1943 when I had pulled several strings to help me on the way towards becoming a Mosquito navigator. The Mosquito was already legendary, even at that early stage in its lifetime, and I was very happy when my efforts were crowned with success.

After about five weeks of crew training, we were posted to 105 Squadron at Marham. Came the evening of November 11th, 1943 . . . Dusseldorf . . . 28,000 feet . . . four 500lb MC (medium capacity) bombs. The tension and excitement of a first operation . . . the power and thrill of take-off with a full bomb load . . . a steady climb to operational height on the English coastline . . . the rush and panic to find two wind checks in 15 minutes . . . and the even worse panic applying those winds to the two remaining legs of the flight plan in the next six or eight minutes. On the run-up to the attack leg . . . switch on *Oboe* receiver . . . listen for the Morse call signal . . . DIT-DA . . . DA . . . DA-DIT DA . . . switch on our transmitter . . . within seconds a succession of dots . . . thank goodness, we've not overshot the beam.

On the attack run the flak started about four or five minutes before target and immediately it was apparent that it was intense and extremely accurate. *Oboe* entailed the pilot flying dead straight and level for 10 minutes on the attack run. Suddenly a tremendous flash lit up the sky about 50 yards ahead of our nose and exactly at our altitude. Within a tenth of a second we were through the cloud of dirty yellowish-brown smoke and into the blackness beyond. I shall never forget the spontaneous reaction of both my pilot and

Safely home. Wing Commander Hughie Edwards VC DFC (later DSO) shuts down after another daylight sortie from Marham. Edwards, who won his Victoria Cross with 105 Squadron in 1941 on Bristol Blenheim IVs, returned to command 105 again on Mosquitos on August 1st, 1942.

myself. We turned our heads slowly and looked long and deep into one another's eyes—no word was spoken—no words were needed. Despite continued heavy flak, we completed our attack run and dropped our bomb load on the release signal, within a quarter of a mile of the aiming point and, with luck, some damage to an important German factory.

Turning for home and mighty glad to be out of the flak, I glanced out of the window at the starboard engine and immediately noticed a shower of sparks coming from the engine cowling. A quick glance at the oil temperature gauge showed that it was going off the clock. Only one thing for it and the pilot pressed the fire extinguisher button and then feathered the engine. The sparking ceased but we now had 300 miles to go and only one engine to do it on. I remember thinking that this wasn't much of a do for our first operation, but at least we had a good deal of altitude and still had a fair amount of speed, even with just one engine. The main danger was interception by a German night fighter and I spent a lot of time craning my neck around to check the skies about our tail. The other thing I remember was a terrible consciousness of my own weight, sitting as I was on the starboard side. However, this feeling wore off and the remainder of the flight home to base was uneventful. Then came the strain of a night landing on one engine . . . again that awful awareness of how heavy I was . . . but after one anti-clockwise circuit, a superb approach and a magnificent landing. I recall the great feeling of relief as soon as the wheels touched the runway. I also remember the urgent desire to get my hands round a jug of beer to relieve the dryness in my throat and to celebrate a safe return from what was to prove my worst experience on Mosquitos. Needless to say, the beer was not long in forthcoming . . .

A quick word with the Technical officer before going to de-briefing. Wing Commander Hughie Edwards VC (facing camera, bareheaded) and his navigator (left) chat with the 'boss plumber' and Wing Commander Roy Ralston (right).

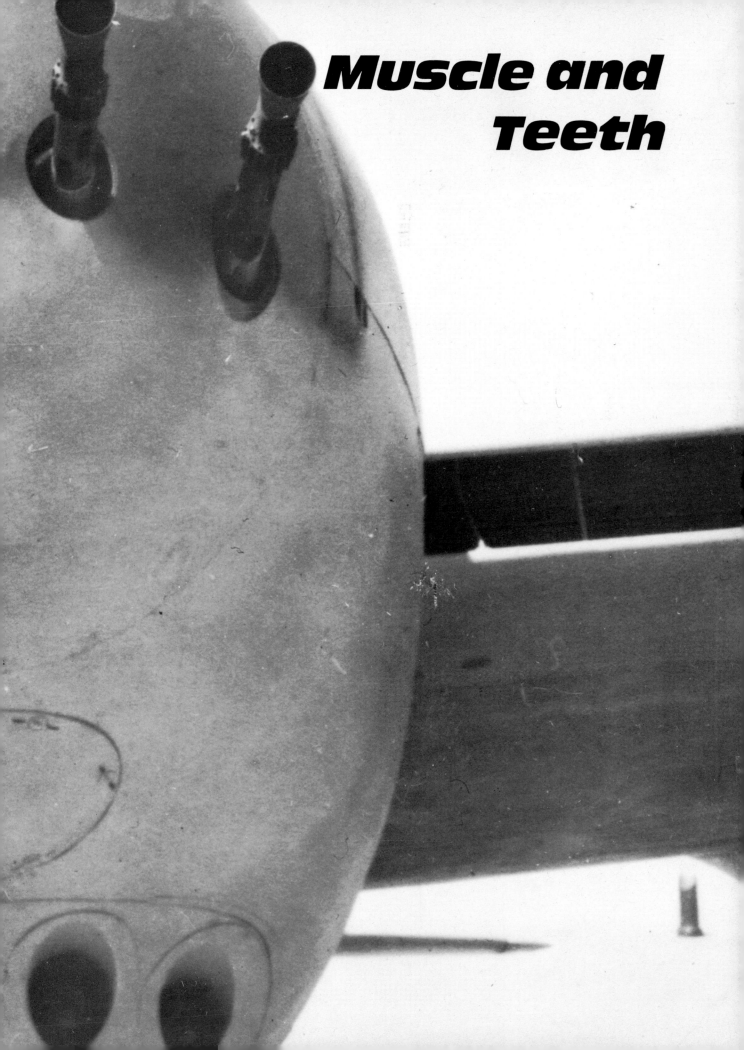

Muscle and Teeth

Above: Butt Test. The deadly sting of a Mosquito fighter amply demonstrated as the four Browning machine guns in the nose and four Hispano cannons are fired together on a stop butt test at night. Fitted to a Mosquito FB Mk VI, the punch of such a battery could be likened to the shock impact of a three-ton lorry hitting a brick wall at over 50mph.

Far left: A closer view of the four 20mm Hispano cannon muzzles, fitted here in a Mk XIII night fighter. The complete dome-shaped ports cover hinged down at the rear, giving excellent access to the Hispanos for removal, servicing and inspection. Further back under the fuselage are the link and empty cartridge outlets.

Left: Bigger and better. The six-pounder (57mm) cannon fitted to the FXVIII 'Tsetse' version of the Mosquito, which replaced the more usual four-cannon armament. After trials at Hatfield from April, 1943, the first two FBXVIIIs, HX902 and HX903, were delivered to 248 Squadron at Predannack, Cornwall on October 22nd 1943 for anti-submarine patrols.

Top right: Mosquito probiscis—the four Browning muzzles protruding from the sharp end of an FBVI. Flash eliminators are fitted to each. Under the belly are the front ports for the cannon quartet.

Right: PZ467, a production FBXVIII 'Tsetse', prior to delivery to an operational unit early 1944.

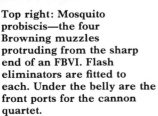

Below right: NT225 (D) an FBXVIII which originally served with 248 Squadron in the summer of 1944, and marked here with the June 1944 'Invasion' black/white striping; displaying its 57mm gun and only two .303 Browning machine guns, these being used for 'sighters' for the larger gun. 100-gallon wing drop-tanks provided the extra range necessary for over-ocean anti-shipping patrols mainly in the Bay of Biscay area.

Far right: It was as a bomber that the Mosquito most amply illustrated its adaptability to extensive modification. Despite its relatively narrow bomb bay as seen here, it was eventually to carry a wide range of explosive stores. The nominal load of two 250lb and two 500lb HE bombs was soon increased on operations.

Above: A 'marker' Mossie about to receive its load of 250lb yellow target indicators (TIs), tail-fused, at Coningsby, mid-1944.

Above centre: The 'Cookie', or more officially, a 4,000lb high capacity (HC) bomb about to be 'digested' by DZ637, a BIV Series II Mosquito of 692 Squadron at Graveley, early 1944. Of its nominal 4,000lb weight, the 'cookie' contained either 2,954lb of Amatol or 3,246lb of Minol 2 explosive filling, according to mark of bomb. Designed simply as a thin-cased can of heat, the 'cookie' relied on pure blast to damage any target, such as a built-up area. The No 2 tail unit (the far-left section here) had no pretensions to ballistic perfection, being basically a counter-weight for aerodynamic balance during its fall.

Top right: Christmas postman. MM199 (Q)—a BXVI—of the Light Night Striking Force of 8 Group (PFF), loading a 4,000lb HC, Christmas, 1944. Take-off and landing with a 'cookie' load required a delicate touch at the controls. Most pilots deliberately used every inch of the runway before attempting to unstick; while the odd occasion when a 'cookie' was brought back demanded a feather-touchdown—usually on a runway distinctly empty of other personnel except for the duty crash crew!

Far left: Going up—a 4,000lb HC bomb being winched into the belly of DZ637, 692 Squadron, Graveley, April 1944. The 'cookie' could only be nose-fused, three air-armed pistols being evident in the nose.

Left: Wing bombs, illustrated here by a 250lb MC, tail-fused HE bomb fixed to a wing pylon carrier on BIV, LR356, 'Y' of 21 Squadron, Hunsdon, in 1944.

Below left: Rockets—four 3-inch rocket projectiles (RP) with 60lb HE heads under the port wing of PZ202, an FBVI fighter-bomber version. This particular Mosquito was utilised for RP and drop tank trials at Boscombe Down in 1945, where this photo was taken.

Above right: Rear-view of the wing RP installation, in this case on a Mossie of 143 Squadron at Banff, early 1945. The long centre-body of the projectile was its individual motor (a 21lb stick of cordite, electrically ignited and thrusting through the rear of the tube). The heads in this tier of RP are 25lb Armour-Piercing—devastating punches against any ship's flanks or decks.

Right: RS625, NE-D of 143 Squadron, part of Coastal Command's Banff Wing, on April 6th, 1945. Normal cannon/machine gun armament is supplemented by only two RP rails per wing, plus two 100-gallon drop tanks of extra fuel. In the nose, an F24 camera for recording results.

418 Squadron. September 30th, 1944. Two Mosquitos. Sqn Ldr Gray (pilot), Flt Lt Gibbons (Navigator); Flt Lt Brook (Pilot), Fg Off McLaren (Navigator), took off from Hunsdon at 1200 hours on a *Day Ranger* to Erding and Eferding.

Sqn Ldr Gray:
Flying about 3,000 feet about the hills en route to our first target, we were jumped from above and behind by two hostile fighters. We ran at full power for the mountains. The fighters closed range to about 1,000 yards, but we managed to shake them in a deep winding mountain pass after a five minutes' chase. A little later, about 50 miles SW of Munich, we saw two single engine aircraft approaching from the NW at 3,000 feet. Our immediate reaction was that they were fighters scrambled to intercept us. We kept our course and passed directly beneath the aircraft at deck level. The aircraft, which we now identified as Me 109s, continued straight on, so we turned and climbed to attack hoping to catch them by surprise.

They probably saw us too for they climbed directly into the sun and were lost from our view. We resumed course for our first target—Erding, which was reached at 1357 hours. Approaching the airfield from the south-east, we spotted numerous aircraft all over the field. We selected two Me 110s parked close together at the western of the landing area. Attacking in a very shallow dive, fired at the nearest aircraft a very long burst of cannon fire and mg. A very great number of strikes were observed all over the engines, nose, port wing root and fuselage, large fragments of aircraft flying off in all directions as it disintegrated. Fire was held to approximately 50 yards. Although this aircraft did not catch fire, we are convinced that it can never be repaired and it is therefore claimed as destroyed. Some cannon strikes were observed on the adjacent Me 110 during the final part of the burst. This Me 110 is claimed as damaged. Proceeding on across the field, another aircraft (U/I,S/E) was spotted at the northern boundary. It was given a 2-second burst of cannon and mg closing to about 40

Day Rangers

yards. Many strikes were observed. This aircraft is claimed as damaged. During the run across the field we were met with a moderate amount of fairly accurate light flak.

Our next call was Eferding which we approached from the north-east at 14.30 hours. Several Fw 190s were seen flying above the aerodrome. We selected one which had its undercarriage down and attacked from its starboard beam. We opened fire with a 2-second burst of cannon and mg from 150 yards. The Fw 190 burst into flames and spiralled into the ground just off the eastern perimeter. This is claimed as destroyed. Another Fw 190 with its wheels down was seen, and approached, but he must have seen us for he raised his undercarriage and climbed almost vertically. We fired a short burst from about 200 yards 40° angle-off (no strikes). Attempting to follow him in the climb, we stalled. The EA did a stall turn and dived to the deck and flew south-east. We resumed the chase and using maximum power slowly closed range. The 190's sole evasive action consisted of flying as low and as fast as possible together with

a bit of porpoising. It was apparent that he was luring us right over Horsching. Hoping to bag him before we reached Horsching, we opened fire with several bursts at extreme range, mainly without effect, until finally a few strikes were observed and immediately my cannon ammunition was exhausted. By this time we were at the north edge of Horsching aerodrome and broke off to the south-west. This Fw 190 is claimed as damaged. At the SW corner of Horsching aerodrome we spotted what is believed to have been a Do 217, which we attacked with mg only. Some strikes were seen on the port wing root and this is claimed as damaged.

By now we were well separated from Flt Lt Brook, we had exhausted our cannon ammunition and in view of the CAVU weather and the great number of 190s which by this time had doubtless recovered from their initial surprise, we dropped our tanks and quickly set course for home. The outstanding feature of the trip was the exceptional navigation of Flt Lt Gibbons.

Below 'Check for damage or deterioration'—the ultimate instruction in most ground trades' servicing schedules. A Mosquito of B Flight 333 (Norwegian) Squadron at Banff gets a 'once-over' DI.

Right: 'Little brother'. A PRXVI, NS569 of the 25th (Reconnaissance) Group, 8th US Army Air Force at Watton in late 1944. Like most American aircraft it carried colourful markings, having an overall PR Blue finish, with complete tail section in red. The white code letter N was carried on a blue circle.

Flt Lt Brook:

We went and attacked an Fw 190 at Erding at 1357 hours. It was parked on the south-east corner of the airfield. We fired about a 5-second burst of cannon and mg closing in from 200 yards to 40 yards. Strikes were seen and the EA disintegrated. Swinging off to port towards the centre of the airfield, we attacked another Fw 190 with a 2-second burst of cannon and mg, closing from 100 to 30 yards. We saw numerous strikes at the wing roots and claim this Fw 190 as damaged. We pulled up slightly and saw an Me 110 parked in a dispersal to the north of the airfield. We attacked this aircraft with a 2½-second burst of cannon and mg from 300 to 50 yards. Strikes were observed on the fuselage behind the cockpit—claim damaged.

At 1430 hours we were closing in to Eferding from the north-east and noticed an Me 109 on the east side of the airfield. I fired a 3½-second burst of cannon and mg and saw strikes all along the fuselage—claim damaged. We then set course for St Dizier.'

On February 16th, 1945, two Mosquitos of the Fighter Experimental Flight, Tangmere, left at 1015 hours for an advanced base in France on a Daylight Ranger to the Vienna area. Crews were Flt Lt P. S. Compton (pilot) and Fg Off S. F. Melloy in the lead Mosquito, with Flg Off K. V. Panter (pilot) and Flg Off J. D. Sharples, DFC, RCAF in the second aircraft. Landing at Juvincourt at 1125 hours, they took off again at 1445 hours for the sortie. This was altered to a Ranger in the Linz area, taking in Bad Aibling, Wels, Eferding and Straubing, as there had been trouble with long-range drop tanks. Just south of Munich, at 1630 hours, Flt Lt P. S. Compton attacked and probably destroyed a truck carrying a large packing case and a camouflaged staff car which was seen to turn turtle. Flt Lt Compton's report continues.

On approaching Bad Aibling aerodrome at zero feet we warned Fg Off Panter that we were now getting near the target area. After receiving his OK, Fg Off Melloy (Navigator) sighted an Fw 190 in the air at 10 o'clock at approximately 1,500 feet altitude. We passed this information to Fg Off Panter and told him to follow us. We made a medium 180° port turn ending up about one mile behind and below the enemy aircraft. At about 1,000 yards range the enemy aircraft started a steep turn to port. We also turned port to attack, closing to about 300 yards and at an angle of about 45° ahead. We fired approximately 3-second burst, seeing strikes on cockpit just below perspex. The enemy aircraft dived down in a port turn. We also turned port and dived after him. The enemy aircraft continued port turn and turned in towards us apparently after sighting Fg Off Panter. We got a 45° astern shot from approximately 200 yards range and at 300 feet height giving him approx-

imately 2-3 seconds burst. My navigator saw strikes on the side of the fuselage and the enemy aircraft rolled on to its back and dived into the ground and burst into flames. We proceeded to set course when told by Fg Off Panter that he was over the airfield and that there was 'bags of joy'. We made a run towards the airfield from south to north and Fg Off Melloy saw an Me 410 (camouflaged blue-grey and dark green) on the ground slightly to port. We gave it a 1-2 seconds burst of cannon from 100 yards range, strikes being seen on port wing and on the ground, and afterwards the aircraft was seen to emit much grey smoke. In the meanwhile Fg Off Panter had made a similar run on an Me 109 to the port of us, which was also observed to emit clouds of smoke after attack. Both Fg Off Panter and ourselves made a second run on both these same aircraft. Our burst struck the ground and then pulled up through the fuselage of the 410. The area was then left and both the aircraft were seen to be smoking. There was slight inaccurate flak (self-destroying) from the east side of the aerodrome. A course was then set for Linz area at 1708 hours and we crossed Wels marshalling yards where we observed six goods trains. We passed east of the town and, observing a number of aircraft parked around the perimeter track. There was no flying here, so we continued to the Straubling area. At 1727 hours Fg Off Panter reported two Me 109s to port over Landau airfield at 2,000 feet. We turned towards them, Fg Off Panter

taking the nearest and ourselves the farthest enemy aircraft. At about 1½ miles range our Me 109 turned hard to port and we followed and at about 250 yards gave him a 90° deflection shot, strikes seen on rear of fuselage, also using .303 when cannon ammunition had run out. The enemy aircraft continued to turn port and dived over the top of us, so we did a steep diving turn to port and saw Fg Off Panter at 45° to our enemy aircraft, which then hit the ground bursting into flames just to the east of Landau airfield. It is believed that Fg Off Panter had also attacked this aircraft. Meanwhile my navigator saw the first Me 109 (Fg Off Panter's quarry) burning on the ground half a mile west of the airfield. Fg Off Panter then turned to starboard and warned us that two Me 109s were overhead at 2,500 feet. At the same time he received a burst of light flak from the airfield (time 1730 hours approximately). Fg Off Panter then called us up and said that he thought he was on fire. We told him that this was so, as we could see black smoke coming from the belly of the aircraft and told him that he should bale out. He immediately climbed to 1,500 feet and both he and Fg Off Sharples were seen to jump by Fg Off Melloy and to land safely 6 miles west of Landau. The aircraft was then in flames and seen to crash. We then set course for Juvincourt. Neither of the other Me 109s made any attempt to attack. Juvincourt was reached at 1930 hours.

Canadian Capers

John Conlin

John Conlin, a Canadian, first joined 107 Squadron in August 1944 and flew a total of 53 sorties before VE-Day. Like most men who flew to war, his memories tend to be clearest on the good times—the parties, the humour and the vivid characters he served alongside. The war may not have been all beer and skittles, but equally it was seldom a high key death or glory routine. Both aspects were experienced in full and yet the perverseness of the human memory prefers to retain the happier moments most clearly.

John Conlin
I met Jim Lee, the squadron intelligence officer, on the occasion of my first operation on August 26th. Being a new boy going out to strike the German Army pulling out across the Seine (as per our briefing), my imaginings of what to expect were fantastic. I expected to see German troops crossing that stream by every conceivable means, from swimming to paddling bath-tubs, and upon arrival found nothing. In fact, I had great difficulty in finding the river for it was as black as seven yards up a chimney, and after I had used up both flares without any

success I was thoroughly lost. Not withstanding a strict admonition at briefing to stay away from Rouen, I approached it unhesitatingly for I did not know where I was, and flew around the biggest bonfire I have ever seen in my life, ultimately dropping two fairly ineffective 500lb bombs and returning to base.

Upon return I was introduced to that delightful custom involving the issue of a tot of strong rum, which the airman issuing it insisted should be taken as a lacing for tea. Not being a tea drinker (not even yet), and having just become a man in my own estimation, I insisted upon having it neat. The rum was duly handed to me in one of those enormous enamel mugs. As soon as I saw the depth of it, I realised that this portion should be treated as suspect. I had a quiet debate with myself on whether or not it should be sunk in one gulp or sipped. Ultimately I opted for the former. The result was catastrophic—tears spurted straight out of my eyes and I was unable to catch my breath for about five minutes, all the while being confronted by Jim Lee, who sat across the table covered by an enormous map, waiting to ask me where I had dropped my bombs, whilst I gasped,

Plug trouble. A Mosquito PRXVI of 140 Squadron, 2nd Tactical Air Force (34 PR Wing) at Melsbroek (Belgium) airstrip in early 1945. In background a Spitfire PRXI.

wheezed and wept. In the long run he introduced himself with the non sequiter 'Am I interrupting you, old boy?'

On another occasion, early in my career with the squadron, being unable to find any suitable target in ten-tenths cloud down to 100 feet, I brought back my bombs and landed with them, much to the chagrin of the ground crew who came up to help with parking in the dispersal and then disappeared pell-mell as soon as they found the aircraft armed. I always thought that was proper when you could fly well for the cost of running the war was high and I felt that aircrew should not be wasteful.

From August 1944 until the end of the war, 107 Squadron was comprised of the most homogeneous mix of personnel I have ever had the pleasure of meeting. Most of the navigators were RAF of English stock, but the pilots were a mixture of RAF, Canadians in the RCAF, Americans in the RCAF, an American in the USAAC, a Norwegian Lieutenant Commander in the Norwegian Navy, a Norwegian Captain in the Norwegian Army Air Corps, New Zealanders and even a South African Air Force Captain, ultimately a Major. Wing Commander W. J. Scott, who had com-

mand of the squadron just before I joined it, was an Irishman who enjoyed sending the boys to South Ireland on leave if he could possibly entice them there in civvies. This crowd operated happily together.

I recall an episode in which a training flight very nearly wrote off the entire squadron. Some clot had the idea that the entire squadron in four flights of echelon starboard, each flight flying line astern, could cross a target and drop the whole complement of 500lb, 11 second delayed bombs before the last kite would be caught in the blast. According to the penguin who dreamed up this exercise, the saturation bombing resulting would be a remarkable improvement over the individual shots that might be made by a single aircraft on a target. In consequence, we were sent on a low-level formation cross-country exercise to end up over the practice target area, all loaded with 12lb smoke bombs. This practice run was led by Lt Commander Skaffhogen of the Norwegian Navy who, when approaching the target,

Covers off at the start of a pre-flight check and top-up. An FBVI of 613 Squadron, late 1944. It was this particular Mosquito in which General Browning, GOC British Airborne Corps, was flown into Normandy in July 1944.

Final top-up of the oxygen bottles which, at maximum gave a six-hour supply. 'W' of 613 Squadron, Lasham, 1944.

found he was off line by about 500 yards to port, and leading 16 planes in echelon starboard and flights in line astern, promptly turned hard starboard to recover, directly into the teeth of the entire squadron, the last flight of which was by that time dragging along the ground in any event. The result was rather like poking a hornets' nest with a stick; aircraft shot off in every direction, over and under each other, some of them practically doing a loop off the deck, the radio all the while issuing choice epithets in the direction of the unfortunate Norwegian and calling his Lapp ancestry into question in strong language. The exercise illustrated, at least to the satisfaction of the pilots, the impracticability of such a venture and we were never called upon to put it to the test.

Squadron Leader Gilliatt had an inauspicious start in the squadron which caused him some concern. As I recall it, on his first trip we were diverted to various stations around southern England as a result of bad weather. The next morning we were expected to get the aircraft back in order that the ground crews could do DIs and have them available for operation that evening. After taking off from hi diversion point, a short distance from Lasham, Gilliatt found the undercar would not come up and immediatel jumped to the conclusion that the groune crew on the diversion field had neglecte to take off the locking nuts. Since i wasn't too far he decided to fly over with the wheels down, but he neglected to select down again before landing and subsequent enquiry revealed that the failure to retract had been caused by an airlock in the hydraulic system. As a result, upon landing the fuselage slowly got closer and closer to the ground, the propellers curling beautifully as they hit the runway; at which point the navigator decided to bale out even before they had come to a halt. He came out through the top of the cockpit and did a better record crossing the infield of the aerodrome than Roger Bannister could, leaving Gilliatt in a blue fog of curses in the middle of the field. The CO was not amused.

Early in October 1944 the squadron had a most successful strike destroying many trains and road transport. We had moved into Nissen huts at Lasham and, since we were stood down the next night, we had a big party to celebrate the event and lord it over our sister squadrons in the wing. Johnny McClurg, one of the Canadian flight commanders at the time (who was later killed in Canada in a flying mishap) decided that the whole episode should be recorded for posterity on the ceiling of the Nissen hut in paint. In order to reach it he had to erect a precarious trestle starting with a ping-pong table, upon the top of which he loaded two other tables of successively smaller size, topping the whole thing off with a chair which formed a platform from which his artistic efforts were carried on. While he was painting locomotives, trucks etc, on the ceiling, black paint dripping down his arm to the elbow, E. G. Smith poured a tankard of beer into his rubber boot (these were necessary in the mud) and McClurg lashed out a kick at him, promptly stepping off perch and hurtling down to shove his foot through the ping-pong table up to the hip. This table, being made of plywood, impaled him and we had to dismantle the whole thing with saws to get him out. This was one of our more successful Mess parties. It's hard to convey the spirit of the moment on paper, although the English cinema has done rather well by it in some of its postwar films.

In like vein were the steeplechases organised by Jock McLeod, the group captain's navigator. Jock was a short man with an enormous walrus moustache. He delighted in getting the entire wing organised in a steeplechase, using all the chairs and chesterfields in the Mess as hurdles and the cushions to pad the fall on the other side. Being short, Jock felt that there should be some form of handicap for taller fellows who could clear a high obstacle, so he used to buy gallons of beer all poured into pint glasses which he would line up along the back of a chesterfield. Following one successful circuit of the 'course' by all contestants, Jock would call a halt until he had brought more beer to pile on top of the last row, continuing this process until a tall and shaky barricade of glass filled with beer confronted the runners. The whole thing generally ended up in a shambles of broken glass, with uniforms and cushions sopping and reeking of beer.

Our squadron navigation officer, Flight Lieutenant Arthur Little, was generally a source of music whose piano playing was almost a religion with him; once at the keyboard it took a lot to disturb him. On one occasion the Mess members had made a pile of furniture and perched the piano on top. At the piano was Arthur Little, playing happily away. Suddenly he smelt burning and on looking down saw that he was 'playing' Joan of Arc as well.

Flight Lieutenant E. G. Smith and I had identical Service careers with 107 Squadron. About the time we had reached 48 trips, a directive came down from headquarters that the tour would be extended from 50 trips (as it then was) to 85 trips, 300 hours or nine months service on the squadron, whichever should first elapse. We were given one month's leave at the end of 50 trips which we spent in England, returning to do three more trips before the expiry of our nine months' service and the termination of the war coincided.

The pilot accepts the aircraft and signs the 700, prior to an air test. 613 Squadron, Lasham, September 1944.

Start of Another Op

Top: Squadron Commanders' briefing. Group Captain Max Aitken DSO DFC checking details with the commanders of Banff Wing's Mosquito Strike units, Wing Commander G. D. Sise, DSO DFC (right), a New Zealander, and Wing Commander R. A. Atkinson, DSO DFC (centre), an Austrialian.

Above: Wing Commander Hughie Edwards VC (left) and his navigator about to board a 105 Squadron Mosquito BIV, Marham, 1942.

Right: All aboard. A 613 Squadron crew climb in at Lasham, September 1944.

Top centre: 'Crew in'. A view which emphasises the compact cockpit seating of pilot and navigator in an FBVI. The navigator (left) was slightly behind the pilot yet still close enough to the controls to take over in any emergency. Protruding from the dashboard (right) at eye-level is the Mk II gyro gun sight (GGS) a distinct but unavoidable facial hazard in the event of a crash landing.

Top right: 'Everything OK, Bud?'. An American crewman has a final word with the pilot before closing the hatch door on a Mosquito PR of 25th Recce BG, USAAF at Watton, February 1945. The last physical contact with the ground is now complete—only voices on the R/T will keep that contact alive for the next few hours.

Right: Knobs, dials and switches. Dashboard of the Mosquito FBVI. The GGS has been removed (empty bracket top centre). Two main throttle levers are at extreme left with black handles; the white-topped lever pair being for RPM Control. The two large push buttons at top right panel were feathering controls. Top trio of pull-down switches were (from left) two radiator shutter and one air-intake filter switches. To their immediate right, the rudder trimming tab and indicator. Just below right bottom corner of the central instrument flying panel are two levers; the left for bomb doors selection and the other for undercarriage. All IFF, TR, fuel and general electrics switches were on the starboard side of the cockpit, by the navigator's right hand (out of view here).

Above: 'Permission to taxy'. Flying control officer in his mobile caravan at Lasham, 1944, in direct R/T contact with the crews.

Right: 'Come ahead both'. An airframe mechanic marshalls the pilot on to the perimeter taxy-track. Dispersal scene of 613 Squadron Mossies at Lasham, 1944.

Below: Taxy-1. Having started engines on the outer fuel tanks, the pilot warmed up on main tanks and begins taxying with full fuel. HX917 of 487 Squadron rumbles across the grass airfield of Swanton Morley, Norfolk on April 7, 1944.

Left: Taxy-2. NFXIII, MM512 of 409 (Nighthawk) Squadron, RCAF raising a dust storm near the shattered remains of a hangar at Carpiquet, France, on August 26th, 1944. The MkXIII carried the Mk VIII A.I. gear in a 'thimble' or Universal ('Bull') nose and carried four 20mm Hispano cannons as its offensive armament.

Middle left: Taxi Rank. Mosquito FBVIs of the Coastal Command Banff Wing (Nos 143, 235, 248, 404 and 333 (Norwegian) Squadrons) thread their way single-file through the dispersal huts to the main start-point. In the foreground, a Percival Proctor IV 'hack' communication type, beyond which are 143 Squadron Mossies dispersed each to its own pan. Even in such sparse surroundings, the British characteristic of making his home his castle is evident in the neatly whitewashed borders to the dispersal garden in the foreground.

Below: Picking Up Formation. Two vics of three Mossies of 464 Squadron RAAF tighten up the formation as they set course for Germany, September 1944.

Top left: 'Twelve men went to mow'—a Mosquito fighter-bomber outfit give the airfield one last beat-up before setting course for the objective. October 1942.

Left: Lone Ranger. FBVI, MM403 of 464 Squadron, RAAF in September 1944, tucks in close to the camera.

Below: 'Web-foot warrior'— Coastal Command Strike Wing Mosquito FBVI of 143 Squadron, RS625, (D), from the Banff Wing showing its pleasing lines at close quarters.

Top centre: Day Ranger. A roving Mossie, its bomb doors still open, wheels away from its own bomb bursts on the hangars of Gael airfield, near St Malo, France.

Above: Pin-point destruction, a particular metier of the Mosquito, exemplified by this on-target shot taken during the 613 Squadron attack on The Hague Central Registry on April 11th, 1944. Led by Wing Commander R. Bateson, six Mosquitos utterly destroyed a single building in a densely-populated city area and returned without loss—in broad daylight.

Left: Fighter Fodder. A Junkers 88 victim of a roving Coastal Command Strike Mosquito in the process of destruction over the Bay of Biscay, 1944.

Below: Ju 88 Confirmed— another victim of a Mosquito's eight-gun punch during a daylight 'ranger' sortie over France.

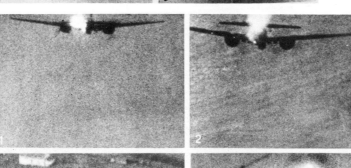

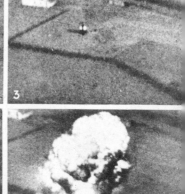

Now Thrive the Armourers...

Jack Simpson

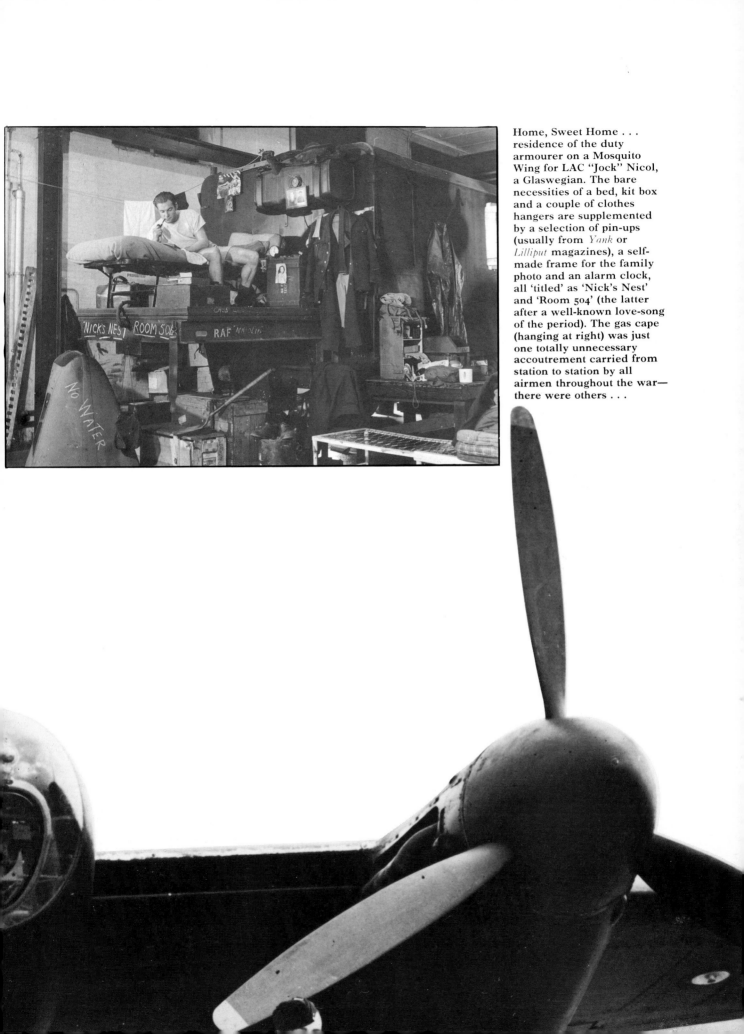

Home, Sweet Home . . . residence of the duty armourer on a Mosquito Wing for LAC "Jock" Nicol, a Glaswegian. The bare necessities of a bed, kit box and a couple of clothes hangers are supplemented by a selection of pin-ups (usually from *Yank* or *Lilliput* magazines), a self-made frame for the family photo and an alarm clock, all 'titled' as 'Nick's Nest' and 'Room 504' (the latter after a well-known love-song of the period). The gas cape (hanging at right) was just one totally unnecessary accoutrement carried from station to station by all airmen throughout the war—there were others . . .

A quick clean for the nose gun bay of Mosquito FBVI, LR 366 (SY-L) of 613 Squadron at Lasham, early 1944. In the background is LR370. Conscientious armourers were almost fanatical about keeping the ammunition boxes' interiors spotlessly clean—a necessary precaution to avoid jamming due to accumulated dirt.

Right: Lapping-in the .303 ammunition belts for the nose Browning guns of FBVI, LR374 of 613 Squadron at Lasham. Each box could hold up to 1,000 rounds, usually in belts of mixed ammunition types, with day or night tracers spaced according to individual taste.

62

Perhaps 95 per cent of all published accounts of the air war tell of the aircraft and the air crews. As the sharp end of the RAF's organisation, this is as it should be. What is not generally recognised is the gigantic backing in personnel, administration and technical service necessary to put one aircraft and one air crew into the air. It's like an iceberg—only the tiny tip stands proud, gleaming in the sunlight above a grey, featureless ocean, but beneath the surface the vast bulk of supporting material maintains that glistening needle-point steadily and constantly. It would be invidious to select one ground trade from all others as being more important—all had their niche in the scheme of things and all were vital in their own way, even if that vitality was often not apparent to the individual 'Erk' involved! If only because of the sheer numbers involved, the armament trade might best illustrate the quality of backing given to the fliers and their steeds. Armament was the largest recruited ground trade of the RAF during the war—despite the common legend that for every 'technical' man, ten pen-pushers grew overnight. And for those who revel in statistics, the armament trade also suffered the greatest proportion of casualties of all main ground trades.

Apart from the pre-1939 regulars, trained at Flowerdown, Eastchurch and Halton, few armourers during the war received what would normally be regarded, in regular Service terms, as adequate training in their craft. The bulk of the trade during 1939-45 were not fitters, but mechanics with knowledge of the ironmongery of their trade, soon supplemented by an ingrained wealth of experience gained 'on the job' at operational units. Their lack of engineering background was not important in the overall picture because all maintenance was checked, supervised and over-signed by the Group 1 tradesman, the fitter armourer, who assumed final responsibility for the work entries in the Form 700's servicing, arming and modification logs. At least, that was the book procedure. In practice, the mechanic was often as good as or even better than the fitter when it came to actually doing the job.

Jack Simpson describes himself as a typical wartime 'plumber'—no promotion, no medals, no glory—and a hell of a lot of blisters. Originally volunteering to become an air gunner, he was rejected medically as being 'too tall and too heavy' and was offered a choice of several semi-skilled ground trades. He chose armament mechanic and after a sketchy training on a variety of weapons ('None of which I ever met again'), was promptly employed in a bomb dump. After a year of 'painting red signs, counting detonators and cleaning the mud off bombs', he was posted to the first-line element of a Mosquito squadron.

My posting was only too typical of wartime journeys. Interminable waiting at changeover stations, crowded carriages with no seats vacant, a crowded corridor infested with kitbags and big boots, and ending at a one-horse country station consisting of one platform, one building—and six miles from the aerodrome. Luckily for me, a three-ton truck had met the train to collect some stores, so I got a lift to the main gate of the aerodrome. On booking-in, I was directed to my billet. This involved a 1½-miles walk along a country lane, passing several isolated Nissen huts in the corners of fields, until I found a rusting Nissen hut marked 'B4' almost

hidden by trees in the near-corner of a particularly muddy patch of greenery. About ten yards from its entrance stood a solitary water pipe with tap, sticking vertically out of a morass of mud and puddles—the billet's sole ablution facility, as I soon discovered. Inside the Nissen hut was one central pot-bellied stove for 'central heating', surrounded by eight beds of sorts.

Waking to a freezing dawn (it was February) I was shaken to be told that I'd better get dressed quick or I'd miss 'the wagon'. It was about 5.30am! A scramble over the tailboard of a consumptive Bedford lorry, driven by the fattest WAAF I'd ever seen, and fifteen minutes later we arrived at the entrance to an oblong, near-white brick building, the cookhouse. Breakfast was spartan—inevitable beans, a fluid red splurge identified as fried tomatoes and a wisp of bacon. A chunk of un-fresh bread, scrape of margarine and a china pint-pot filled with viscose brown tea. Back to the fat WAAF and after weaving our way through a maze of hedgerows and dirt tracks, the Bedford suddenly threw out the anchors and the driver informed us that we had arrived at B Flight dispersal 'All off, B Flight'.

The aspect of B Flight, my future place of employment, was sparse. Two huge,

inverted engine transit boxes, standing duty as flight offices, one elongated Nissen hut, a hard-standing of crumbling tarmac on which were parked a gaggle of trolley accumulators, some plain wooden hand-carts (our ammunition transporters), half-a-dozen issue bicycles, two bomb trollies and one ancient Austin 'Matchbox' car, this being the pride and joy of Flight Sergeant S - - - - - , the 'boss' of B Flight maintenance crews.

'Chiefy' resided in one of the ex-engine cases, its open doorway being surmounted by a neat board announcing 'NCO i/c', and after reporting to him, I was sent to the armoury—one end of the long Nissen hut. First impression of the armoury was confusing—it looked like an ironmonger's jumble sale. Bomb hoists, known as 'hockey sticks' because of their vaguely similar shape, carriers, SBCs, ammunition boxes, cannons and belt-feed mechanisms—all stacked, hung and

A short wait for the electricians and engine mechanics to complete their own pre-flight checks before moving in with the bomb loads. A gaggle of 500lb MC bombs about to be loaded to 487 Squadron FBVIs at Swanton Morley, April 8th, 1944. Aircraft here is LR355.

Left: A posed view of the cannon bay of an FBVI but illustrating the excellent access afforded to armourers for loading/unloading or removing/installing cannons.

63

Below: Winching up the wing bombs—a 250lb GP bomb being hoisted to its pylon carrier by means of hand winches known colloquially as 'hockey sticks' for obvious reasons. Although this was the 'book' procedure armourers quite often humped the GPs up by their own muscle to save time—a not altogether safe way of going about the job . . . Aircraft is LR374 of 613 Squadron, September 1944 at Lasham.

Bottom: Once hooked in position, the bomb is 'crutched down'—a simple screw-down of two pads for keeping the load rigid on its pylon. The transit plug in the bomb nose indicates a tail-fused store, implying a delayed action detonator fitted internally.

cluttered around the walls. A few wooden trestle tables served as work benches, a row of pegs to one side held several shabby greatcoats and rainproof mackinaws. No one seemed either surprised or delighted at my arrival. Finally, I was spoken to by a chubby-faced youngster with very blonde curly hair whose pink cheeks seemed innocent of a razor blade's touch. (I was all of 24 years of age at that time.) This 'kid' turned out to be my corporal!

Life on B Flight had a simplicity of purpose that is hard to recall accurately in the sophisticated world of today. We worked to all hours, there was no laid-down working hours or normal routine. A seven-day week, every week, with an occasional scrounged 36hour pass and, very rarely, even a few days leave. The daily round quickly became a familiar grind. DIs (daily inspections) first thing, sign up the bumph, then wait for Chiefy to find out about the night's ops. By late morning we usually had some idea of what was on and the bomb dump wallahs would

be beavering away preparing the 500 pounders or, quite often, 4,000lb 'cookies Once trollied, these were tractored down t our (and other) dispersals and left for u to load. Meantime we'd be getting the gu ammunition ready, checking, positionin in the belt machine and lapping into th narrow boxes. Air tests were soon com pleted and we'd do the after-flights an pre-flight checks ready for the actual ops

Once the engine and electrician trade had finished, bomb doors were opened an the armourers moved in. Run in th trollies, hooks lowered, hoist, lock an check. Safety fusing wires in position safety pins to stay in until the aircrew came out, sign up the arming log in th 700, a quick tidy-up and then relax on th grass with a smoke and the latest *Lilliput*

Before long out would come the crew and each nav and pilot made their ow internal and external checks. Hand th bomb safety pins to the navigator. Whe satisfied, the pilot signed the 700 accepting the aircraft. He was now responsible fo bringing the Mossie back in one piece t

us. We seldom stayed to see them off—when you'd seen one Mossie take-off, you'd seen 'em all—and left that chore to the airframe lad shepherding them out to the perimeter track. We were more interested in the pot of tea waiting for us at dispersal, brewed in readiness by the duty armourer.

The only air crew I came to know by name and sight well were the squadron and flight commanders. The flight commander in particular always made it his business to drop in to Chiefy's office for a chat most days and, occasionally, popped his head in to the armoury for a quick word and a cup of tea. Once back in the armoury, the duty crew settled down to wait for the return of the aircraft, while everyone else gathered their belongings—all in one small webbing side-pack, the badge of any dispersal 'erk'—and were soon bouncing their way back to the cook-house on the back of the transit lorry. By then it was usually too late for thinking of an evening out—in any case there was nowhere to go, other than the village, a sleepy collection of houses, cottages and one pub, about three miles across the fields. Even a visit to the NAAFI canteen meant a long trek along the lanes from our billet—we seldom bothered. About once a month, if ops and duty allowed, as many of B Flight as possible put on a clean collar and assembled in the public bar of the village pub for a beer session, although these were strictly groundcrew occasions.

Thinking back, I've probably presented a pretty gloomy view of our life. In fact, it was a happy time for me, in spite of fairly primitive living and working conditions which would turn a modern trade unionist's hair grey . . .! We were a close bunch on B Flight and felt apart from the remainder of the station. When I finally left on posting to a peacetime station, with all its comparative luxuries of brick billets, hot baths and beautifully maintained grass verges, not to mention the 'bull' on station parades every week, I felt even then that I'd never again know the real team spirit we'd had on B Flight dispersal.

A big one for Berlin. Lining up a 4,000lb HC 'cookie' with the bomb bay of Mosquito BXVI, PF432, ('W') of 128 Squadron at Wyton on March 21st, 1945—one of the 139 Mosquitos which raided the German capital that same night. March 1945 saw Mosquitos bomb Berlin on 27 nights, a total of 1,222 individual sorties which cost the loss of seven Mosquitos. The transit plugs in the nose of the 'cookie' would be replaced by arming pistols once in position for hoisting.

Another cookie carrier receives its load, DZ637, a BIV Series II (modified) of 692 Squadron at Graveley, PFF, early in 1944.

Cat and Mouse
Hal Bufton

By 1942, Bomber Command had come to
realise that despite the early years of
optimism and unbounded faith in its men
and equipment, actual results of bombing
left much to be desired. Statisticians and
chair-borne experts may have given glow-
ing reports of devastation caused in
Germany, but the crews knew better.
With out-dated equipment, bombing
accuracy was more a matter of pure luck
than judgment and the tragically mounting
roll of casualties was not justified by the
damage caused. New, accurate, instruments and black boxes were desperately
needed if Bomber Command was ever to
play its true role in the air offensive.
Equally needed were new aircraft to
replace the pre-1939 outmoded designs
which, though playing a sterling role, were
simply behind the times. Four-engined
'heavies' had begun re-equipping front-

line squadrons—and, though its real potential was recognised by only a relative few, the Mosquito was about to commence its meteoric career.

One of the new scientific aids to accurate bombing was *Oboe*—a simple system of radar transmitters, based in England, which could direct a pilot on to any target within its range and then indicate a precise bombing release point. Though initially *Oboe* had certain limitations of range and manipulation, it was accurate to a degree hitherto unknown—and, most important, could be used in practically any weather conditions. Therefore, added to the efficiency and performance of the Mosquito bomber, a new era in bombing seemed possible.

Hal Bufton was one of the first men to prove the superb ability of the Mosquito as a bomber spearhead employing *Oboe*. Despite hamstringing from certain higher authorities and the inherent dangers of the early trials of any 'new' weapon, Bufton and the few other crews of 109 Squadron proceeded to demonstrate that, given reasonable backing and a fair measure of good fortune, *Oboe* could add teeth to the bomber offensive. For the first time the men of the bombers could be reasonably sure that their sacrifice and unquestioned courage would not be squandered on fruitless sorties.

It was 109 Squadron's Commanding Officer, Wing Commander C. C. McMullin, who was the man who produced the final gleam of genius to put the four main facets of *Oboe* together—the principle of a target-finding force, Coxen's target indicator, Reeve's *Oboe* and the Mosquito—and one week before the final decision to begin installation of the Wellington VI on a production basis, he got hold of a Mosquito and installed all four bits into it just in time for the conference, which accordingly rejected the Wellington in favour of the Mosquito. It was a most happy result and one which gave us the thing we needed most—a large degree of immunity on operations. If the German had been able to recover an *Oboe* set from a crashed aircraft, the run of the system would have been very short indeed. As was, it appears almost certain that they did not capture a set until early 1942. With the successful application of *Oboe* and the decision to use the Mosquito in the summer of 1942, two flights of 109 Squadron, which had been dealing with investigation of German radar and counter measures against German beam bombs were split off and 109 was realigned as purely an *Oboe* marking squadron.

We moved to Wyton as the first Pathfinder squadron in August 1942, began to equip with Mosquitos and build up our crew strength from the original three. We should have been ready to start work by about October but ran into a snag with *Oboe*. Up till that time we had only flown it in Wellingtons at heights of up to 10,000 feet. We found that in the Mosquito one of the radio valves regularly blew up at little over 20,000 feet. After some small detective work, Reeves and his colleague from TRE found the trouble lay with a small electric motor (from the Hoover vacuum cleaner) used to drive a cooling fan which speeded-up at altitude and got into resonance with the valve. They cured this problem in time for us to begin operations during December. There were no other fundamental faults with the *Oboe* sets after that, I believe, but we were always subject to technical failures of up to 30 per cent.

We did the first *Oboe* operation with Mosquito MkIVs on December 20th 1942 against a coking plant at Lutterade in eastern Holland. At that time we had six operational crews and eight aircraft. Four more crews were trained by January and by June 1943 we reached about 20 crews. In July 1943, 105 Squadron was linked up with 109 as the second *Oboe*

68

squadron and a few of their existing crews were trained on *Oboe*, while the rest of them joined 139 Squadron and became the first of the Mosquito Light Night Bombing Force. About half of the 20 crews of 109 Squadron moved to 105 and half the ex-105 *Oboe* crews came to 109. By the end of 1943, 109 Squadron crew strength had again increased to a full strength of about 20 crews. It is interesting to note that the official history, *Strategic Offensive against Germany*, reports (p128, Vol 2) that only five 109 Squadron crews were lost up to the end of 1943. That is, we only lost one quarter of our force which is a striking tribute to the performance of the aircraft. As I believe it, only one of these was positively identified as going down over Germany, with the possible loss of security to the system.

As already mentioned, the first *Oboe/Mosquito* operation was done against a coking plant at Lutterade, East Holland by six aircraft on December 20th, 1942. It was supposed to be a virgin target, completely clear of bomb holes, and we were intending to use it as a calibration target for checking *Oboe* accuracy. When we got the photographs about three days later we found the attack had been useless as a calibration as the target was smothered with bombs from some earlier attack which had hit this target in error. We subsequently had to set up a further calibration effort which was done on a small German officer cadet school at St Trond, near Florennes, Belgium on February 15th, 1943. From memory this had previously been a Belgian boarding school and appeared to be a medium-sized country house, probably about 30 or 40 yards square.

We had four aircraft on this target and apart from photographs which showed that we had some direct hits, we received a detailed intelligence report from a man on the ground who gave us the exact location of the bomb hits. As far as I remember we had three or four hits on the school which killed a sentry at the gate and two officers in their rooms. Significantly, it was also reported that two separate bombs from different aircraft had landed a kilometre from the target. We were not sure how authentic this report was and we played down these loose bombs at the time. Which was unfortunate as later on similar results cast doubt on the *Oboe* system. In the Florennes attack two aircraft had dropped their bombs in salvo. This was our regular practice when marking so that the TIs covered the smallest area possible.

At that time we did not know that when bombs were dropped in salvo, frequently two of them hit each other with a high risk of one of them spinning and falling back. We were not aware of this happening during the Ruhr attacks of 1943, probably because the fires started were so intense and the normal driftback of the attack obscured the odd stray marker which might fall short.

However, during the pre-invasion sorties in the spring of 1944 where the targets were mainly railway yards and only high explosive (HE) bombs were used by the main force, errors stood out. I remember one case at Tergnier in April 1944 where we had one aircraft using the Mk1 *Oboe* system with reds and one using MkII with greens (TIs). The MkII system was still experimental at that time—hence the difference in colour and reds were the primary markers. It developed that both aircraft marked at just about the same time. The reds and greens were about 400 yards apart, as we had suspected they might be, but in each case one of the four markers had fallen back by nearly a mile so the result was a rectangle marked by three reds at one corner, three greens at another and a red and a green at the others. Results of this sort tended to destroy confidence in *Oboe* after that and a master bomber was introduced to assess the accuracy and, if necessary, report the TI to attack. If we had only studied the results of the Florennes calibration earlier we would have resolved this gap in the RAF's technical knowledge before the main bomber offensive got under way and saved a lot of grief. As it was it was not until May 1944 that we did the necessary trials ourselves on a bombing range which showed that bombs dropped in salvo might cause trouble.

This is going off at a slight tangent, but on one major attack on flying bomb sites in north France in April 1944, nine targets were marked with *Oboe* reds only and all attacks were successful. A tenth target— the 5 Group one—was marked by *Oboe* with yellow proximity markers with the intent that these would be followed up by a 'Newhaven' marking technique of illumination and final identification and marking by the master bomber. Unfortunately, the illuminating flares did not go down on time, the master bomber could not identify the target for a long time and in the end his reds went down about 30 minutes late. There were about 120 Lancasters on the target which was three miles inside the French coast. During that half-hour alone we saw 20 shot down. These were the only aircraft lost out of a thousand-plus operating on flying bomb sites in the area that night. To make it worse, the target was not hit.

We followed up the first *Oboe* attack on Lutterade by further HE attacks against Ruhr targets for the remainder of December 1942. 'Ding' Ifould and I were one of the crews from 109 on Essen on December 23rd and on Hamborn, December 24th. This last one was interesting. Up till that time there had been no damage of any consequence done to Ruhr targets due to the heavy defences and constant smog. On the night of December 24th one of the crews, Somerville and Maas, had a small malfunction which resulted in a delayed bomb release of about three seconds (600 yards). On

Christmas Day, 1942, Lord 'Haw Haw' reported that the RAF had carried out a 'terror' attack on Christmas Eve but had only succeeded in hitting a cemetery at Hamborn. We checked the maps and sure enough there was a cemetery 600 yards south of our target—just where we calculated Somerville's bombs had hit. Presumably the rest of us—whose equipment worked correctly—must have hurt quite a bit.

By the end of December we were ready to mark targets. The weather over Germany, however, was against us and continuous cloud cover prevented the first ground marking until March. Our AOC Don Bennett, thought up a skymarking technique which we tried out on December 31st for the first time with a small number of follow-up aircraft of PFF acting as main force bombers. We dropped bundles of coloured parachute flares at some height— say 10,000 feet—above cloud level. The follow-up bombers would approach on a pre-determined heading and aim at the markers. There were big errors in the system, the principal one being the drift down-wind of the marker flare. With a 60mph wind at flare height, the flare would drift three miles during the time it was burning ie it would be between one and one and a half miles off target at start and finish. Despite these limitations *Oboe* skymarking was spectacularly successful compared with the strictly negative results achieved on the Ruhr prior to this and was used on a number of nights during January-February 1943. Ifould and I did seven sky-marking trips to the Ruhr in January.

An interesting development early in January was an instruction from Bomber Command that *Oboe* Mosquitos were to stand by to lead daytime formations of Lancasters against the Ruhr. It was one of those utter stupidities that develop in war from the intense drive to 'get on with it'. We had the potential with *Oboe* to enable

Bomber Command to write-off the Ruhr; but we were operating on a shoe-string; we needed highly trained and experienced crews—we had only 10 or 12 with only one flight of aircraft. *Oboe* could be jammed within a few days if the Germans captured a set of equipment. Yet the Bomber Command C-in-C's determination was such that he was willing to risk losing use of the system during the whole of 1943 just to get in a few relatively small-scale daylight hits during the bad weather winter months.

The idea was that the *Oboe* aircraft would lead the formation at about 23,000 feet and, after crossing the coast, would climb above the formation to 28,000 feet to make the bombing run. The Lancasters were supposed to bomb when they saw the bombs leave the Mosquito a mile above them! We had one formation practice with about 100 Lancs of 1 Group on January 9th which was a disaster. However, we stood by for this folly for several weeks until our representations to Air Ministry resulted in a clamp-down on the Command which resulted in *Oboe* Mosquitos being restricted to night-time marking operations only. This was almost as bad from our angle as the C-in-C's plan as it meant that we could not train our new crews by giving them practice with HE before they were let loose with markers. *Oboe* Mosquito-led Lancaster formations became practical in late 1944 when the ground stations were based on the Continent and the shorter range allowed attack at 15-20,000 feet.

The first *Oboe* ground-marking effort was made on St Nazaire on February 28th, using the experimental ground stations on the South Coast. We had only one *Oboe* channel, so our risk of failure was high. As it happened the first marker aircraft succeeded by the skin of its teeth and the two or three backers-up all failed. The markers were right on target and huge damage to the town's dock area resulted.

It was the first time one of the French ports had really been hit despite numerous attacks by Bomber Command and within a few weeks further 'area' attacks on these targets were prohibited to prevent further damage to the French. St Nazaire was the first full trial of the *Oboe* Mosquito in its ground-marking role and proved a resounding success.

The first time ground-marking was used against a German target was on Essen on March 5th, 1943, and the second on Essen again on March 12th. From then on until the major attack on Hamburg in July, practically all Bomber Command's effort was concentrated on the Ruhr—with 109 Squadron *Oboe* Mosquitos marking. After July we were not called on so frequently as the Ruhr began to receive lower priority. At the same time German jamming became more of a problem since we were still using the Mk1 system. We continued to be successful until November 19th when we had our first complete failure, due to jamming, on Leverkusen After that we were of little use until the flying-bomb targets came up in January 1944, leading to the pre-invasion interdiction programme on rail yards and the later close support for the army. By this time we were using MkII *Oboe* and also could use Mk1 as we were away from the areas of jamming in central Germany. The 10 coastal gun sites on the invasion coast were marked with *Oboe* on June 6th, 1944 for the follow-up attack by the full Command. Afterwards *Oboe* Mosquitos were used for marking in close support of the Army. They came back into their full strategic role against German targets in the autumn of 1944, using ground stations in Belgium and France which extended their range to Berlin.

Our operations were strictly a team effort. Each of the two *Oboe* channels we normally had available could work only one aircraft every 10 minutes. In 1943 a full-scale Command attack of 600-1,000 aircraft took about 40 minutes. Our plan was normally for one channel to mark at H-2 minutes, H+8, H+18 and H+28; the other channel at H, H+10, H+20 and H+30. We had a failure rate of about 30 per cent which gave us, perhaps, an 80 per cent chance of getting one of the two aircraft successfully on target at each 10-minute interval. That is, of the aircraft at H and H+2 which started off the attack, we could only expect 80 per cent success. Since that first mark was the be-all and end-all, we laid on a heavy system of back-up. We put a reserve aircraft on each channel which went in with the leader and stood by (about 7-10 minutes from target) waiting to replace any failures. In addition, the second and subsequent aircraft on each channel went in 10 minutes early, so that it could take over the time slot of the aircraft ahead if it and the reserve both failed. This gave us six chances of getting the first mark down on time and, until Leverkusen, we did not fail. However, there were a few occasions where we were a minute or so late when the reserve or second back-up was called after failure of the lead aircraft late in the proceedings. Usually, even if the reserves were called in, we managed to keep timing within 30 seconds. With our concentration on getting the mark down at H-hour, we often missed at H+10 or H+20 spots— but never (I think) both of them. Since the TIs lasted only three minutes in the early days (six and 12 minutes later on when a proportion of delayed candles were used), there were big gaps between the Mosquito red markers even when our programme was perfect. These holes were filled up by the Lancaster markers of PFF which covered our reds with green TIs and kept the pot boiling. *Oboe* by itself would rarely have worked. It needed the follow-up of the rest of PFF.

Despite its ceiling the Mosquito could not fly high enough for longer range targets—we would have needed a satellite.

As a solution to this a system of *Ob[oe]* repeaters was developed, whereby a rel[ay] aircraft patrolled a line joining the groun[d] station and the target. This could ha[ve] increased our range up to about 6[00] miles. It was a very complicated syste[m] and failed to get enough high-level suppo[rt] to ensure its full introduction (by which [I] mean that the opposition was stron[g] enough to squash it). We had one repeate[r] working at the end of 1943 and did on[e] operational trial against Emden. One *Ob[oe]* leg was direct from East Anglia and th[e] other, via repeater, from Dover. I se[e] from my log that Squadron Leader B[ob] Findlater and I flew this trip on Octobe[r] 24th, 1943 in a MkIX Mosquito, LR49[?]. We were trying out the very complicate[d] system of radar routings and relays throug[h] our two aircraft, the repeater and th[e] bomber. For the sake of form we had t[o] have a target and the gate to the dry doc[k] was selected. We heard later that we hit i[t].

The individual sortie consisted of [a] climb to height from base to the Englis[h] coast. From there we flew at our operation[n]al height, 28-30,000 feet, to the start of ou[r] bombing run, about 50-60 miles fro[m] target. We had *Gee* over the North Sea s[o] that our navigators could get extra ordinarily exact timing. Our bombin[g] runs were 10 minutes long and were alon[g] arcs of circles centred on either Dover o[r] Caistor. For most of the Ruhr we use[d] Dover for our tracking station which gav[e] us a north-south run. For Dusseldor[f,] Cologne and Wuppertal etc, we tracked o[n] Caistor on a North-east bombing run[.] Whenever possible we chose the north[-] south run as it was usually down-wind an[d] gave us a ground speed of 400+mph an[d] sometimes as much as 600mph. The 10[-] minute run was straight and level, so w[e] appreciated the speed of the Mosquito[.] Our biggest trouble was with flak. Sinc[e] we were straight and level, almost alway[s] from the same direction, and ahead of th[e] main bomber stream, we were a nic[e] exercise piece for the gunners. They developed an efficient plot system of gun control which frightened us all but did not produce too many losses. For the last three or four minutes of our bombing run, we were the centre of concentrated fire. We could always see it; sometimes from behind reflected in the side blisters—which was good. Sometimes ahead, which was bad. Sometimes we could hear it, which was worse and sometimes smell it as well, which was awful. The usual practice was to put the seat down as low as possible so that you could not see out and do the run on instruments—it was like putting on blinkers. We frequently had flak holes and often lost an engine due to splinters. The Mosquito did not seem to mind. Flak holes were patched in a few hours with a fabric patch or simple carpentry repair. Engines could be changed in 3-4 hours after the crews got the hang of it. It was easy to get back on one engine even if on some of the landings one went astray.

With an aircraft of such performance, fighters were no great worry, but I believe we lost a few to lucky fighters—they *had* to be lucky to cope. It was sometimes disconcerting to be following a series of, say, five condensation trails of the aircraft ahead of you and to have an extra trail from a fighter join in for the rest of the trip. Still, so long as the trail was in front, you were safe. We required crews of very high ability to give the responsibility, skills and consistent determination needed. I believe that, above all, the Mosquito gave us those crews. We had a free hand to recruit anyone in Bomber Command during 1942 and probably we could have any willing customer from anywhere in the RAF. We were very lucky in our initial recruiting—later on the Mosquito did the recruiting for us when the news got around.

We got Mark IX Mosquitos about May 1943. I flew LR496 on May 29th, 1943. The MkIVs were terrific, but the IXs were fantastic. It was a tremendous boost to fly an aeroplane without fear of icing—those winter thunderstorms over the North Sea were now below us—and with the certainty you could get back on one engine. Even better, that a minor crash, like hitting a haystack and traction engine at full circuit speed resulted in gentle disintegration of the aircraft, splinter by splinter, with the crew walking safely away (this happened!). While enough can never be said of it as an operational aircraft in 1943-44, it should be said that the Mosquito had a few minor snags. These were its tendency to swing on take-off and landing. These faults were much pronounced on the IXs and XVIs and when the paddle-blade props came along with consequent increase in critical speed, they became a source of some trouble in single-engine landings to us, in our ignorance of those days. We lost a few crews due to these faults, but without them the aeroplane would not have given us the near-immunity we needed on operations. Roundabout trips, most times, easily outweigh a few swings. I never met a Mosquito crew that was not thrilled to bits with its aircraft from 1943 on.

Some mention should be made of the Mosquito/Lancaster value ratio. A figure of 3 to 1 is sometimes quoted. The Lancaster cost three times as much as a Mosquito and had a crew over three times as big. It carried three times the bomb load, but for only one-third of the sorties ie an average tour of 20 sorties per crew compared with 60 for the Mosquitos. What is left out of this picture is the experience of the crews. The Lancaster crews had average experience of 10 trips at any one time and were thus almost always half-trained. The Mosquito crews had an average experience of about 30+ trips and had a far more satisfactory performance. For an *Oboe* Mosquito, carrying a 4,000lb bomb, the ratio would be almost 50 to 1.

Intruders- The Night Stalkers
Ernest Gates

Perhaps the loneliest role of the Mosquito was photo reconnaissance—unarmed, unprotected, relying only on surprise, speed and sheer daring to penetrate an enemy's defences and unfold his secrets. Almost on a par with those courageous men of the PRU units were the Intruders. Two men in the cramped panoply of cockpit piercing the stygian blackness of night to prowl over enemy airfields and communications. Once airborne, the Intruder crew were literally on their own. As their Mosquito diminished into the gathering dusk of England, their identity became merely a blip on the baleful eye of an RDF (Radar) set—their names chalk marks on a peeling operations board, alongside a cryptic four-figure number denoting take-off time. The moon was their natural opponent, inky blackness their friend. All the black boxes conjured up by boffins could not replace their own observations—eyes could pick up the instant flicker of a house light carelessly exposed, the orange glow of a railway engine scurrying through the night or the blue-red sparking trail of an exhaust pipe on a German aircraft about to land at its base. It was a sneak

thief war in which **success** came from hitting an opponent in the back when he was least expecting it. An enemy bomber on finals after a gruelling trip, its crew thankfully relaxed and preparing for landing, would suddenly experience sheer terror as a cacophony of exploding cannon shells ripped into their aircraft from behind. By the later stages of the war the Luftwaffe in Europe became almost obsessed with the daring of the Mosquito intruders. Two ironic phrases were born— '*Moskitopanik*' and '*Ritterkreuzhohe*'. The first summed up the constant awareness of Mosquitos ever-lurking in the vicinity, waiting to attack them over their own flare paths; while the second phrase (literally, Knights Cross Height) described wanly the only reasonably safe method of escaping death on take-off by flying at zero feet across the adjoining countryside until well clear of the ubiquitous Mosquitos. Intruders usually had specific areas or purposes to cover—diversion attacks, bomber escorts or plain enemy airfield blanketing during heavy bomber raids. In February 1943 a slightly different form of intrusion, called *Ranger* was gradually implemented. *Ranger* aircraft were literally free-lance operators, out of touch with home stations and left to their own devices to cause as much chaos and disruption as possible among the enemy. Whereas Intruders had specific areas or objectives to prowl, the *Ranger* Mosquitos literally looked for trouble. Both forms demanded the same qualities from crews— boldness, resolution and a determination to seek out and destroy whatever the odds or circumstances.

We spent three months at the Mosquito OTU at Bicester where most of our flying time was related to low-level cross-country experience. Very few hours were devoted to night flying and yet, on posting to 613 Squadron at RAF Lasham, all my operational hours except about four were spent on night intruder flights. Learning on the job I think they call it today!

Although Lasham airfield during the summer of 1944 was similar to all other wartime stations in that there were several dispersed domestic sites and Nissen huts for the Messes, top-level administration compelled us to live under canvas. We

were told that on eventual transfer to the Continent after D-Day we should be required to take all our accommodation with us. The German scorched-earth policy would leave nothing of the airfields from which we were to operate in France. Therefore, experience of living in tents was 'vitally necessary'. So, for many months, we squelched about in rubber boots, tried to shave in luke-warm, smoke-impregnated water and wore clothing that frequently got the mildew in our rather damp travelling cases. Needless to say, on arrival at Cambrai/Epinoy in the autumn of 1944 we found the aircrew quarters, recently vacated by the Luftwaffe, to be rather better that the average Nissen huts on the airfields back in Britain. Certainly, they were centrally heated and did not rely on temperamental coke stoves for warmth.

I well remember my first operational flight with my pilot, George Topliss. It might more fairly be described as the night operation that nearly never was. The task was to patrol a small area of northern France in the Amiens-Beauvais area. After meticulous flight planning and adopting all the techniques with which I had been drilled at OTU. I was ready to depart. George went through his pre-flight checks with more than usual care and eventually we were airborne. Crossing the Channel was peaceful enough and then we saw the French coast darkly outlined against the sea ahead of us. Acting as he had been instructed, George commenced evasive action to confuse the enemy aircraft and flak. Unfortunately, his action confused us more than the enemy. My pilot later admitted that he scared himself to death as he nearly lost control with his over-violent manoeuvres. Busy in my endeavours to maintain checks on our directions, I was unaware of the situation. Ever after that we simply took no evasive action whatsoever on crossing the enemy coast, and on no occasion did enemy guns open fire as we entered their territory. We certainly have lived to tell the tale which nearly was never told because of my pilot's enthusiasm to follow his flying instructors.

At the other end of the scale there was the occasion when 613 Squadron was given a stand-down so that we might celebrate our 2,000th sortie since D-Day. A great party developed, officers bringing their wives and 'popsies' from all corners of the country. On the understanding that there would be no operations task given to the squadron on the morrow, everyone had a thoroughly good time, eventually seeking rest in the early hours either in damp beds out on the airfield or with human hot-water bottles in hotels in nearby Alton. To everyone's horror Steve, the squadron adjutant, came round about mid-morning on the following day trying to rouse heavy-headed aircrews who were expected to be airborne by two o'clock in the afternoon.

After much searching and the making of many telephone calls, the adjutant found the required number of personnel to man six aircraft. In my case, as both my pilot George Topliss and I were bachelors sharing the same tent, we were able to fly together on this low-level daylight raid on Egletons in central France. A number of the other aircraft had very mixed crews. The only common feature about us all was the alcoholic haze which threatened to reduce our vision and perception. Slowly we collected our thoughts and struggled through briefing. Eventually we became airborne about two hours late. However, merely to prove that aircrew did not require boisterous good health for the success of a flying mission, the result of our raid on a French technical school, currently being used by the German Gestapo, was a tremendous success. Only one aircraft was shot down and its crew reached the safety of the Allied lines on the north side of the river Loire.

'Mothers' Meeting'—Scene at the Pathfinder Force Headquarters, Wyton each morning as AVM Don Bennett presides over the start of another night bombing operation.

I grew very fond of the Mosquito in which we carried out most of our first tour operations. The two ground crew were also very proud of the aircraft and did everything in their power to maintain it in near-perfect state, often under appalling conditions on the dispersal. As each operation was successfully accomplished, I felt that I owed something more to the machine itself, rather than to the men who serviced it, and a kind of dependence on it for survival developed in my mind. Each time as we thundered down the runway at the start of another trip, I settled into my seat with a complete sense of security and I accepted that 'K' for 'King' would see us through another mission. Looking back on it now I become rather embarrassed at my naivety of thought but, at the time, it felt reassuring as one placed one's faith blindly in a complicated mass of machinery. The persistent, powerful drone of the engines, a steady vibration through the warm, snug cockpit, the pale opalescent glow of the instrument panel and the green flickering haze from the GEE set all created a special tiny microcosmic world of their own. We seemed completely separated from the reality of the earth below and the war in which we were engaged. I suppose I was subconsciously recreating the security of the womb. However, I never had the same feelings in other aircraft and I can only conclude that it was the neat efficiency of the Mosquito and its cockpit layout which led me to this secure state of mind.

It really never occurred to me that I was flying in a wooden box with all the associated frailties of plywood. As the aircraft roared across the enemy countryside, our small secure and powerful world seemed detached and immune from the worst terrors that the enemy could produce. Nevertheless, this is not to say that I was not afraid. Every time George dived towards our target into the midst of the colourful streams of anti-aircraft fire, I sat immobile, anxiously counting out the altimeter readings and suddenly realising that my heart was thudding heavily against my ribs. There was the natural excitement of the situation, but there was also the fear. Does any man knowingly place himself in a position where the

possibility of death in its most horrifying form is there before him and not feel some kind of fear? A number of incidents still vividly stand out in my mind and the following typify my feelings at the time.

One pitch dark night we were patrolling in western Germany and spotted a small light immediately ahead of us. Working on the principle that any light in blacked-out Germany was always worth attacking, George immediately pushed the nose down and lined up to make a cannon attack. In actual fact we were unfavourably placed to make this attack, being too near the target and too low in altitude. Steeply we rushed in, the altimeter lagging danger-

Top: Briefing—the 'navigators' union' of a Mosquito Wing at Banff check out details of route, times, courses; apparently to Norway according to the map of the navigator in the foreground.

Above: *Oboe* Mossie—DK333 'F' one of the early BIV Series II Mosquitos to equip 109 Squadron, the pioneer *Oboe* unit. Named *Grim Reaper* this was the mount of Fg Off H. B. Stephens and his navigator, Frank Ruskell; seen here with their ground crew. Stephens was later killed in action.

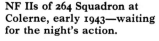
NF IIs of 264 Squadron at Colerne, early 1943—waiting for the night's action.

ously. Suddenly the reading dropped dramatically to 500 feet, which was the height of the ground in these parts. Clapping George on the back, I yelled at him to pull out. He did so and, as we levelled off and then quickly commenced to climb, the dark silhouettes of trees rushed past the aircraft on the starboard side. We must have been merely a split second from disaster and oblivion on that occasion. For the remainder of that intruder trip our actions were far from enthusiastic and daring.

On another occasion we decided to work as a pair of intruders with another aircraft in the squadron, piloted by Frankie Read. He was to drop the flare over the town of Venlo when we were favourably placed to take advantage of the illumination. Thoughtlessly we forgot that we too would be lit up and that we would present a splendid near-daylight target to the enemy gunners. There we were at about 1500 feet above Venlo, naked under the yellow light of Frankie Read's flare and near-blinded by its brilliance. Not so blinded were the German light AA gunners and almost immediately we were engulfed by a

tangle trellis of coloured tracer shells. Identifying nothing and with the instinct of self-preservation uppermost in our minds, we dived rapidly away from the light of the flare into the comparative safety of the stygian blackness of night beyond the town. Once again we trembled to ourselves and decided to use greater prudence in any future combined attacks.

One night we were called upon to patrol an area in eastern Holland. The intruder trip itself was uneventful and we saw nothing worthy of serious attack. So, dropping our bombs on a secondary target—a railway marshalling yard—we set off for home at the end of the hour-long patrol. Rather than fly over enemy-held Belgium and France as we made our way back to Lasham, we decided to cross the Dutch coast near Ijmuiden and seek the relative safety of the open North Sea route. Passing over the coastline we suddenly found ourselves enveloped in heavy cumulo-nimbus cloud. One minute we had been sailing across calm untroubled skies and then the next we were immersed in apparently endless masses of black turbulent cloud. As the aircraft writhed

'G-George away'. 139 Squadron Mosquito BIV roars over a companion at Swanton Morley.

and creaked in the terrifyingly violent air currents, George wrestled with the controls to maintain the aircraft on an even keel. He dared not attempt to turn to escape the way back we had come through fear of the aircraft being thrown on its back; so he first tried to climb out of the storm. The rain and hail spun off the propellers, the inherent charges of static electricity making them glow like huge Catherine wheels. Then we heard the clatter of ice against the fuselage as chunks broke off the blades. Down went the nose as George tried a second plan to fly beneath the storm. However, the up-currents were so powerful that the aircraft continued to go upward all the time.

After what seemed an interminable period of terror, we suddenly broke out of the cloud at about 16,000 feet. The tortured groaning of our sturdy little Mosquito ceased as she found herself flying once more through untroubled air. My own memory of that moment of peace after the anguish and strain of the previous ten minutes will for ever live in my mind. We were now flying down a huge valley of sky between mountains of cumulo-nimbus.

A half-moon illuminated the turret tops and massive towers of cloud in a cold, pale glow. Black, fearful shadows were cast in the depths beneath us. It was a Himalayan fairyland. We had just escaped from the dark, terrifying dungeon of the ogre's castle and were now sailing serenely away on the wings of our gallant wooden saviour.

On this occasion I, as navigator, swallowed my pride and permitted George to call up Manston for a QDM. After quarter of an hour when it was nearly impossible to keep any kind of air plot, I thought it prudent to accept outside aid. In actual fact the course I had given my pilot after our ordeal was almost identical with that obtained from Manston control.

A less terrifying but nonetheless apprehensive moment occurred when we were told to patrol the railway systems running into Hanover. The night was very dark with low cloud scudding across the sky in a strong westerly wind. I faintly discerned certain landmarks which enabled us to locate a marshalling yard somewhere on the west side of the city. We dropped a flare at about 1500 feet just below the

included many humorous episodes. There was the time we tried to 'borrow' the parrot from a pub in Odiham; trying to help George Topliss, a great hulk of a chap, into bed after his getting blotto on champagne, losing my Service Dress hat and finding it a forthnight later under the mattress of his bed. I suppose one could write a volume about one's personal contacts and the relations that were built up over the months.

In the Mosquito two-man crews the relationship grew very close; not like the larger crews where the situation in a bomber aircraft did not encourage the same growth of intimate friendship. We on 613 Squadron (and no doubt on other Mosquito units) worked, flew and enjoyed

Top: Take-off. Trim elevator to slightly nose-heavy, rudder a touch to right and ailerons neutral . . . fuel cocks fully on . . . props to max. revs . . . flaps up . . . radiators open . . . straighten tailwheel . . . throttles open slowly . . . watch the swing . . . brakes off . . . let's go . . . plus 9 boost . . . 150 knots . . . trim to tail heavy . . . climb at plus 7 and 2650 revs . . .

Above: Time To Go . . . Flight Lieutenant R. D. Walton (left) and F/Sgt Bill Harper get in.

cloud base and made a turn to port trying to identify something worth attacking. We had not allowed sufficiently for the strong wind and, by the time we had completed the circuit and were coming up to the flare, it had drifted a considerable distance towards the east. Peering ahead searching for the target, we were in fact skimming over the rooftops of the centre of Hanover. Apprehensively we waited for the trigger-happy Germans to let fly at us, a naked sitting target in the light of the flare. Miraculously not a gun was fired and, as we climbed rapidly into the thick cloud, we heaved a sigh of relief. I rather think we dropped our second flare with greater care that night.

The happier side of squadron life

our leisure together and, naturally, a close friendship grew up between certain crews. In addition, the camaraderie usually divided up again into pilot and navigator associates.

On stand-down periods we usually collected together in the Mess bar. Life on the squadron was one of some strain and the only release for one's tension and pent-up feelings was to seek refuge behind a pint of beer, a game of darts and conversation. Sometimes we would gather with the other fellows of the squadron and slowly a party would develop quite spontaneously. They were tremendous fun on account of this spontaneity, quite unlike the rigid present-day guest nights when one is expected to be in a party

spirit to order. There was an air traffic controller, whose name now escapes me, who was a wonderful pianist. Prime him with pints of beer and he would lead us in a sing-song. It may sound rather tame entertainment compared with the sex-ridden stuff of this 'sophisticated' modern era, but the songs were far from subdued. 'Salome', 'Eskimo Nell', 'The Ball of Kirriemuir'—all came in for regular treatment and I blush now to think of the obscenities which I sang so gustily with all the others. As we tired of this kind of entertainment some enthusiasts would challenge the rest to party games. 'High Cockalorum' was popular and forward rolls over the Mess furniture required a skill which one apparently possessed only

Below: Dusk take-off for MkXVIs of Bomber Command Light Night Striking Force—target, Berlin.

Bottom: 'Minions of the Moon'—Night fighter crews of 605 Squadron have a final chat before take-off, Castle Camps, May 1943.

after several jugs of ale. In the cold, sober
light afterwards we wondered why no one
had broken his neck. Other activities
centred around a pile of Mess chairs up
which crews were compelled to climb in
order to write their last successful operational exploit on the roof of the Nissen hut.
Slowly one scaled the furniture and then,
precariously perched at the top of the
pyramid, pilot and navigator would daub
a picture of a train or similar enemy target
on the ceiling with the date of the action.
Immediately on successful completion of
this acrobatic exercise, well-intentioned
fellows below assisted you down by pulling
away the chairs at the bottom. About
11 o'clock after such evening beer parties,
we healthy young aircrew by this time
were fairly hungry. Someone would
suggest a night-flying supper so off we'd
dash to the Airmen's Mess where a 24-
hour service appeared to be arranged for
flying crews. I well remember a flight

commander of 107 Squadron—anothe
Mosquito squadron on 138 Wing—goin
off on his own for such a supper on
perishingly cold winter night. He neve
made the Mess and was eventually dis
covered the following morning curled u
fast asleep in a snow-drift. Needless t
say, he spent many days in hospital re
covering from pneumonia.

The reality of life was often brough
home to us at the termination of a
operation. Frequently, fellows with who
one had shared the previous evening
entertainment were posted missing. Fc
me the thought of being shot down neve
entered my head. I suppose it was in
evitable that one thought 'it's not going t
be me'. If one had not thought this wa
one could not have carried on. Every cre
member in a Mosquito squadron wa
known to the others and each time on
aircraft went missing, we all felt the los
Nevertheless, one carried on and left it t

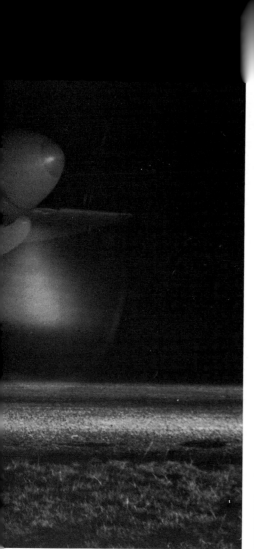

the Commanding Officer and his adjutant to write the usual letters to bereaved parents and wives. However, I was seriously disturbed by the loss of Ronnie Elvin, a navigator. He and his pilot went missing on a patrol over Germany in the autumn of 1944. Ronnie and I were great buddies and we had a lot of similar interests. Very often we would walk out into the countryside and chat about home, life before joining the RAF and what we intended to do 'after the war'. On such excursions when we were stationed at Epinoy, we would end up at a small estaminet on the road to Cambrai. There we practised our schoolboy French and helped the patron to drink some pre-war vintage champagne which he had hidden successfully from the Germans for four years. Afterwards, with fuzzy heads and full of bonhomie, we would stagger back to our billet, arms locked together and singing all the popular choruses from Vera

Thimble Nose—HK428 ('K'), a Mk XIII of 29 Squadron, fitted with A.I. Mk VIII in a slim nose radome. K-King joined 29 Squadron on January 28th, 1944 and claimed the destruction of a Junkers 88 on the night of June 17th, 1944.

Lynn's latest hits. Then suddenly it was all over. A gap appeared in my routine and, for the first time in my life, I realised what it meant to lose for ever a true friend.

It might not be inappropriate to conclude these reminiscences with a story that concerned neither death nor glory. George Topliss and I were on a night-flying test from Lasham one day early in 1944 and therefore only expected to be airborne for a few minutes whilst we tested the Mosquito and its equipment. Consequently, I did not take a map or list of call-signs for other flying stations in the vicinity. Unfortunately, as we made our final approach to the runway, a rain squall came across the airfield. Hastily, the air traffic controller sent us away to another airfield. He gave us a course to steer, a distance to fly and the call-sign of the diversionary airfield. Turning on to the heading according to the directional indicator, we flew off calling up the airfield, the name and location of which were unknown to us because I had no list of call-signs with me. We could not compromise the airfield over the R/T by asking for its name in plain language. We flew for a period of time to cover the distance quoted and saw no airfield ahead. Only then did George realise that he had set his directional indicator to zero as he had lined up on the runway for landing at Lasham and we had flown off in a direction which took us anywhere but along the route given by the controller. Correcting this error, George called base again for a QDM, only to be told that the weather had closed in and we were diverted to yet another airfield, of which we were given the call-sign. We did as we were told and eventually flew out of the rainstorms to see an airfield ahead. We eventually landed there and you can imagine our shame as we stepped out of the Mosquito to ask the ground crew at what aerodrome had we landed. It turned out to be Dunsfold and we found ourselves having to spend the night in the Mess in battle-dress and flying boots. We looked a sorry, unshaven sight on the following day when we finally returned to Lasham after a 'short' night-flying test which lasted 24 hours. On all future flights, whatever their duration, I took everything in my navigation bag, including a shaving kit.

Bomber Support-Operation Flower

Flower was the code-name given to the overall role of Bomber Support by fighter Mosquitos and was intended to nullify German night fighter interference with main bomber forces' efforts. It could be called a logical extension of the then existing Intruder and Ranger roles. From December 1943, Mosquitos of 2 Group and other Intruder units became required for *Flower* sorties. A *Flower* operation usually consisted of two phases, the first being bomb-carrying Mosquitos ahead of a main bomber force to raid Luftwaffe bases in an attempt to keep their night fighter force grounded; while behind them came the long range Mosquitos who 'policed' known night fighter bases by patrolling in the vicinity, waiting to bounce any aircraft taking off or landing. At 1030 hours each morning, the duty intruder controller would contact Operations 2 at Bomber Command Headquarters to see if *Flower* operations were needed that night. If so, the DIC passed a preliminary warning to the squadrons, via their respective Group Operations Rooms and

ound out how many aircraft could be made available. As soon as the main Bomber Command plan became available —usually at about 1230 hours—the DIC would prepare his own plan for the night's operations. After his plan's approval by Group Captain Operations 3 (or his deputy), the DIC notified all units concerned by secret telephone. Final approval of the plan would be given at the Intruder Conference held every day at 1430 hours and any changes notified to units by secret telephone.

Individual station commanders were given the final responsibility for briefing crews and, particularly, for deciding if the weather conditions were suitable. Providing the Intruders could take-off from base, and even if it was certain that they would need to return to other bases due to a predicted clamp in weather at home base, the aircraft could be despatched. Forward UK bases usually used for *Flower* included Bradwell Bay, Ford, West Malling, Coltishall, Manston and Hunsdon. All

Flower aircraft were necessarily fitted (with IFF (Identification Friend or Foe), Mk IIG or Mk III; while VHF radio transmitters had frequencies allocated by parent Groups.

Another form of Bomber Support for the Intruder and Ranger Mosquitos was Operation *Distil*. Early in 1943 the Luftwaffe began to employ specially-equipped Junkers Ju 52 aircraft for mine-sweeping in certain coastal areas around Europe, usually from first light on days following any suspected Bomber Command *Gardening* (mine-laying) sorties. These Ju 52s were known colloquially as *Mausi* aircraft. Ranger and Intruder Mosquitos were soon called in to combat the *Mausi* Junkers, 605 Squadron being the first unit to be so employed after May 1943. While a Junkers 52 was no match for a Mosquito fighter, the real dangers of a *Distil* sortie lay in the fact that it took place off the enemy-occupied coastline, in broad daylight, and a Mosquito crew could often expect the *Mausi* aircraft to be escorted by Luftwaffe fighters.

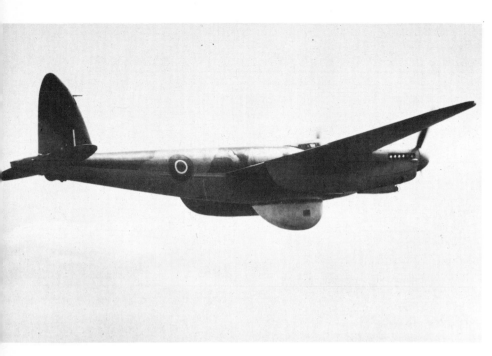

The target flew over the top of the airfield, orbited to port, gradually lost height from 5,500ft to 2,500ft. I followed down to 3,000 feet, when my navigator informed me target was making off in a northerly direction. I followed target which flew at varying heights between 3,000 and 6,000 feet and closed range to 600 yards dead astern. Visual was not obtained due to poor visibility, so I lost height placing myself 200 feet below target which was then slightly to starboard when a faint visual was obtained. I closed still further to 300 feet to positively identify target, continuously calling 'Bogey, Bogey, waggle your wings' and navigator interrogated with IFF. To this there was no response. At 300 feet, I obtained a visual on a Ju 188 and asked navigator to confirm independently.

We both simultaneously identified target as a Ju 188 which was flying at 4,000 feet with speed of approximately 240mph. I then increased range to 600 feet and pulling up dead astern opened fire with a 3-second burst, closing in from 600-300 feet. The port engine caught fire enveloping the wing in flames which broke off from the

Eyes in the Dark. A B MkXVI fitted with a special H2S radar 'black box'. Usually the spearhead of the PFF Mosquito Force, H2S-equipped Mossies were first used operationally on February 1st, 1944 when Berlin was the target.

On November 21st, 1944, Pilot Officer Beynon (pilot) and Pilot Officer Pearcy took off from Hundson on *Flower* at 1845 hours, bound for Sachsenheim aerodrome. The pilot's report reads:

The English coast was crossed at Manston on way out at 1905 hrs landfall being made on the French coast at Calais, 1913 hours. The route to target was uneventful, patrol area being reached at 2032 hours. The weather at the target was 9/10ths stratus base 1,500ft and visibility was very poor. Through a break in the cloud the airfield was seen lit with red perimeter lights. The patrol was continued on DR with the aid of the aerodrome beacon visually flashing 'VG' and seen occasionally through breaks in the cloud till 2047 hours when contact was obtained.

I was patrolling Sachsenheim airfield at 4,000 feet on an east-west patrol line on the north side of the visual beacon when my navigator obtained a contact at 2¼ miles range, crossing from starboard to port, slightly above whilst on a vector of 090° M. I immediately turned to port on vector of 310° M behind bogey, increasing speed to 270mph. Giving chase, I gradually closed range to 3,000 feet, when I observed ahead and to port an airfield which was fully lit with V/L and red perimeter lighting, on the west bank of the Rhine. This we later assumed to be Spayer Airfield.

fuselage. At the same time an explosion occurred in the cockpit which set the fuselage blazing. The EA rolled over on its back and dived vertically into the ground where it blew up with a violent explosion and burnt at 2008 hours. I estimated my position to be West of Ludwigshaven at time of combat. I claim 1 Ju 188 destroyed thanks to persistent work on the part of my navigator.

Wing Commander F. N. Brinsden, a New Zealander, had fought as a fighter pilot over France and through the Battle of Britain during the first two years of the war. After a spell as a flight commander with 485 Squadron, flying Spitfires, he joined 25 Squadron to pilot Mosquitos. On the night of August 17th, 1943, in support of Bomber Command's devastating attack on the Peenemunde missile site, Brinsden was patrolling the area near Sylt and decided to bomb the airfield there.

We determined to fly out to sea, at about 2,000 feet, as though flying home, then descend gradually, still heading westwards until at sea level, about-face and fly back to Sylt, hoping by these means to outwit the radar screen and carry out a surprise attack. All went well.

As we approached Sylt pinpointing was easy for the town was silhouetted against a clear sky and the full moon made the scene as light as day. Over the town then at roof height, a slight turn to port towards the aerodrome hangars shining in the moonlight at about half a mile away, range shortening, coming up to optimum—stand by—bombs gone. Now a vicious turn to starboard to pass between the hangars—and blindness. A searchlight shining right into the cockpit instruments; nothing to help us orientate ourselves, and too low to evade vigorously. Then tangerine tracer shells passing too close to be safe. Now something had to be done. Violent evasion—and at sea level—while still heading generally eastwards was the only course open.

At last the searchlights were lost and the tracer stopped but before vision had fully returned a violent acceleration, a dreadful shuddering, broken airscrews screaming. We had touched water—and bounced. Warning my navigator to pre-

Fat Belly. A BXVI, its bomb bay bulged to accommodate a 4,000lb HC 'Cookie' bomb, drones across a sea of cotton-wool clouds. With the moon lighting the scene, Mosquito crews continued to be astonished by the sheer beauty of such a cloudscape —though such circumstances offered ideal visibility to prowling Luftwaffe defenders too.

Bomb Gone—MM220. (X-X-Ray) releases its bulky load of a 'cookie'.

pare for a ditching I meanwhile scanned the cockpit. Rev counter needles were against the stops but other instruments seemed normal. Would it fly us home? Too soon it became evident that it would not and pre-ditching action was taken. The ditching was normal and I had some seconds in which to gather vital papers before the aircraft sank. Then swam towards the dinghy and joined my navigator who by this time was sitting in it. A quick survey of our position showed us to be between Sylt and the mainland and south of the railway embankment joining the two.

Fortunately neither of us was seriously injured. Little could be done to manoeuvre the dinghy. The type we had was a beast of burden, not of navigation, and although we rigged our seat type dinghy sails and endeavoured to sail out of the bay and westward under a favourable off-shore breeze, dawn brought an inshore one and a change of tide, and back we went into the bay. Finally at the mercy of another inshore breeze we were blown inshore at

mid-day on the 18th into an encircling ring of troops, who were impatiently waiting our arrival, having watched us drifting up and down the bay for the last six hours!

On January 28th, 1945, Flying Officer A. T. Sherrett (pilot) and Flight Lieutenant K. MacKenzie, both Canadians, of No 406 Squadron took off from Manston at 1740 hours on a high level intruder sortie to position 49°50N 08° 30E in support of a Bomber Command raid on Stuttgart.

Fg Off. Sherrett:
We left the English coast at Manston, striking directly to target area by DR, GEE being poor at fifteen thousand feet. En route, at 1845 hours, a V2 was seen about 30 miles past Brussels, travelling up very fast in a course of 250°. Patrol was begun in target position at 1925 hours at 15,000 ENE and WSW in relation to beacon *Otto*. Weather was cloudy below 15,000 with haze up to 18,000.

enemy aircraft started to roll, went over on its back and spun straight down. We pulled out at 15,000 and did a port orbit to watch him going in, the target hitting the ground and bursting into flames at position, 48° 34N 06° 33E at 2050 hours. This was confirmed by Flt Lt Honeyman of 151 Sqdn (*Sneezy* 44) who immediately took the fix.

The chase had lasted 45 minutes at full bore, the speed on closing in for the visual at 27,000 was 265mph indicated. After the chase we discovered we had only 60 gallons of petrol left, about 20 minutes flying time, so I throttled back to minimum revs and boost. I gave a *Mayday* on Channel C, asking for fix and homing. We were answered by *Baggage*, an American sector GCI who took a fix and gave us a vector of 140°. We challenged this and received the wrong answer, but as it was in a decidedly American voice and little else could be done we obeyed and were brought into Croix-de-Metz aerodrome at 2135 hours. All fuel gauges registered zero. *Baggage* did an excellent job of getting us in and every available comfort was extended to us at the aerodrome. We returned to base at 1325 hours on the 29th.

Top left: Bomber's Eye View —the fearful scene over Karlsruhe at the beginning of a main-force attack. At top left a cascade of shimmering TIs adds to the 'brew-up'—pyrotechnic markers in brilliant hues that earned the paradoxical nickname of 'Christmas trees' from the German population.

Top right: Munich night scene, December 21st, 1944.

Bottom left: Munster—'all lit up like an illuminated street map', as one pilot described the view at de-briefing.

Bottom right: Dresden, February 21st, 1945, as the fire-storm was reaching its peak.

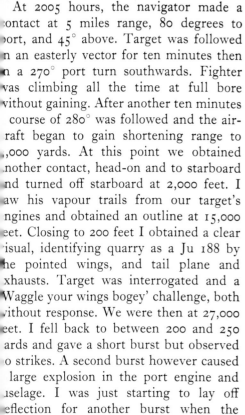

At 2005 hours, the navigator made a contact at 5 miles range, 80 degrees to port, and 45° above. Target was followed on an easterly vector for ten minutes then on a 270° port turn southwards. Fighter was climbing all the time at full bore without gaining. After another ten minutes a course of 280° was followed and the aircraft began to gain shortening range to ,000 yards. At this point we obtained another contact, head-on and to starboard and turned off starboard at 2,000 feet. I saw his vapour trails from our target's engines and obtained an outline at 15,000 feet. Closing to 200 feet I obtained a clear visual, identifying quarry as a Ju 188 by the pointed wings, and tail plane and exhausts. Target was interrogated and a 'Waggle your wings bogey' challenge, both without response. We were then at 27,000 feet. I fell back to between 200 and 250 yards and gave a short burst but observed no strikes. A second burst however caused a large explosion in the port engine and fuselage. I was just starting to lay off deflection for another burst when the

How They Came Back

Right: Return at Dawn—a 29 Squadron FBVI lets down at Hunsdon at the close of another night stalk.

Middle right: On finals . . . check fuel tanks . . . radiators open . . . brakes off . . . wheels down and locked . . . flaps on full . . . . . . revs 2850 . . . speed 105 knots . . . watch the descent rate . . . throttles ready for more power on the undershoot . . . settling now . . . we're down. To go round again, a Mosquito would climb happily at about 120 knots with flaps and wheels down at climbing power. Throttles had to be opened to plus-9lb/sq. inch boost, flaps put to 15° with re-trim as the undercarriage was raised until final attainment of a safe height when flaps were then fully retracted. One-engine landings were reasonably safe providing pilots remembered that the undercarriage took at least 30 seconds to come down at 2850 revs and sink rate increased rapidly as wheels were lowered.

Below: PRXVI NS591 of the 25th BG 8th USAAF landing at Watton on February 22nd, 1945. To go round again with only one engine was not a healthy pastime, but provided ample height was in hand, speed was not less than 135 knots and flaps were less than 15 degrees lowered, it could be done reasonably safely. A flapless landing was very flat and usually made at 110-115 knots with a rock-like control of the airspeed, resulting in a long landing run.

Right: De-brief. Squadron Leader T. McPhee (nearest) and Flight Lieutenant G. W. Atkins of 464 Squadron RAAF (both were English) explaining their night's activity to the squadron intelligence officer at Gravesend airfield, June 1944. At that time, this team had completed 74 sorties together.

Far right: 'He exploded into the ground about there'— Night intruder crews checking location of a claimed 'kill'.

Above: HR241, ('M') an FBVI bomber support Mosquito after a sortie on November 3rd, 1944.

Left: Checking the damage. Wing Commander John Wooldridge, DFC DFM, commander of 105 Squadron, checks battle scars on 'The Joker', the unit's so-called 'gremlin kite'. To judge by the expressions of the crews, the damage was not serious. Marham, June 28th, 1943.

Above: Bonfire Night, 1944— a 29 Squadron Mosquito which crashed on landing at Hunsdon after a sortie over Germany. The crew got out unhurt.

Right: First Operation. MM133 ('D') of 692 Squadron, piloted by Flight Lieutenant J. A. R. Leask on his first Mosquito sortie, a raid on Berlin, March 24th, 1945 was caught by a German nightfighter whose cannon fire caused this tail damage, severed elevator cables and shattered the rudder and elevator tabs. To get home, Leask had to use 10-15 degrees of flap and full right rudder to maintain level flight for the whole return trip, fore and aft trim coming from judicious use of the flaps.

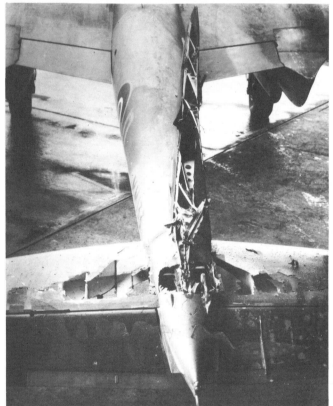

Left: Wing Commander F. W. Hillock (left) and his navigator, Flight Lieutenant P. O'Neill-Dunne of 410 Squadron, Coleby Grange with Mosquito NFII DZ726, (RA-Z). During a patrol over Apeldoorn on the night of April 15th, 1943, the Mossie hit some overhead copper cables, 300ft of which they brought back with them.

Top right: Belly-Flop. HR549, a MkVI of No 1672 Conversion Unit, Yelahanka, India which dropped its port wing tip during an approach and landed 'too low.'

Above: The result of getting too close to an opponent. Flying Officer E. R. Hedgecoe's fighter on March 25th, 1944 after destroying a Junkers 188 the previous night. The explosion of his victim scorched the skin off his aircraft and temporarily blinded him. 85 Squadron at West Malling.

Right: Another victim of 'pressing on', NS960, flown by 605 Squadron's commander, Wing Commander N. J. Starr, DFC and his navigator, Pilot Officer J. Irvine. The enemy aircraft (EA) exploded less than 50 yards away from Jack Starr's aircraft and a piece of the EA's rudder pierced the Mosquito's fuselage almost jamming the controls.

Top and right: Two views of Pilot Officer Beckett's crash at Bradwell Bay, April 1943 when the Mosquito became uncontrollable during landing, ploughed straight through a Nissen hut and hit a searchlight. Both Beckett and his navigator, Flight Sergeant Smith were, amazingly, unhurt.

Below: Bird Strike. One of the hazards of low-level flying amply illustrated here by RF650 of 1672 Conversion Unit, Yelahanka, India after collision with a 10-feet wing-span kite-hawk, July 30th, 1945.

Top: Yet another 'McIndoe job". Flight Lieutenant M. A. Cybulski, RCAF (left) and Flying Officer H. H. Ladbrook with their distinctly 'toasted' Mossie, DZ757 (RA-Q) of 410 Squadron, Coleby Grange after destroying a Dornier 217 on the night of September 27th, 1944. Cybulski had to feather the port engine and return, virtually without rudder control. Each man received a DFC.

Above and left: 'Repairable' — BIV. MM401 after a raid on February 21st, 1944. Hit by enemy nightfighter cannon fire, its port engine was shattered, hydraulics severely damaged and the starboard wing tip smashed. But it came home.

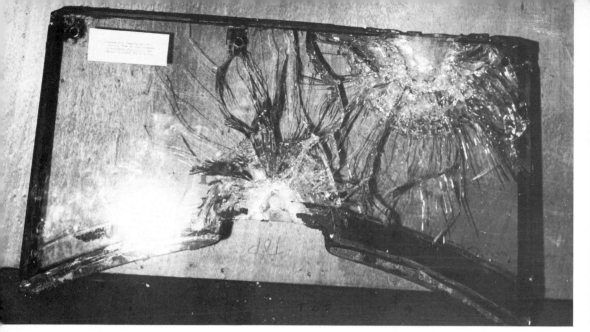

Above: Near Miss. The windscreen of Wing Commander John Cunningham's Mosquito XII after an encounter with a Junkers 188, February 1944.

Top right, Here we go Again. Whatever the condition in which the Mossies came home, it was the ground crews' job to get them serviceable again if possible. LR366, ('L') of 613 Squadron, Lasham and LR370 (background) get a going-over in spring, 1944. LR366 was eventually lost on September 17th, 1944, when, as L of 107 Squadron, it was shot down during an attack on German barracks near Arnhem.

Right: Back from Ops—a 464 Squadron FBVI HX977 at Hunsdon gets a minor-inspection on its Merlins at dispersal. Minors were normally carried out in hangars, but 'needs must . . .' on occasion.

Below right: Corporal N. L. Kingston tussles with the exhaust manifold of a 464 Squadron Mosquito at Hunsdon.

Left: Meanwhile, back in the hangar . . . P. S. Linsell, an ex-chauffeur/mechanic, clearing snags in the gun bay of an FBVI.

Below: 29 Squadron engine fitter at work on a starboard Merlin at Hunsdon, September 1944.

'Achtung Moskito'

Wilhelm Johnen

What was it like to be on the receiving end of a Mosquito 'bite'? Wilhelm Johnen was a Luftwaffe pilot who knew only too well. From his first night kill on March 26th, 1942 over Duisburg until the end of the European conflict, Johnen flew over 200 nightfighter missions, claiming a total of 34 victories and receiving a Knight's Cross for his prowess. In this account he describes his last victory, on the night of March 16th, 1945 when RAF Bomber Command raided Nuremburg (for the eighth time) and Würzburg (for the first time). The several references to a 'tick-ticking' in his head-phones were to the rear-warning *Naxos* radar apparatus of his Messerschmitt Bf 110. Paul Mahle of his crew was credited with originating the upward-firing cannon installation of many Luftwaffe nightfighters—the so-called *Schräge Musik* (Slanting Music)—although an elementary form of this armament was first used by German night fighters in 1918.

'*Achtung, Achtung!* Enemy bombers will be overhead in a few minutes. All lights out. Immediate action stations. Mosquito attack is to be expected. Careful on taking off.' At last the engine started and long white flames poured from the exhaust pipes. Schoppke pushed the throttle forward and the machine bucked. I jumped on the wing and slapped my leading mechanic on the shoulder. I taxied to the start. 'Lobster from Thrush 1—I'm taxiing to the flarepath. Please light up when I give full throttle. Switch off as soon as I'm airborne.' 'Victor, Victor,' replied Lobster. 'Look out for Mosquitos. Good Luck.'

I taxied in the dark and took my place on the runway. I gave her full throttle. The flarepath lights went on and were switched off as soon as I was airborne. I had hardly levelled out when Mahle shouted, 'Look out, Mosquito!' I thought as much. The Tommies had waited until the fish was on the line. I hedge-hopped over the fields and shook off my pursuer. My crew breathed with relief. We'd made it. On the tactical waves we heard new enemy reports. Suddenly there was decisive news. 'Achtung. Bombers are flying in direction of Nuremburg. Moderate-sized formation reported over Ulm making for Würzburg.' I thought for a moment. Nuremburg or Würzburg? I decided for the latter and changed on to a northerly course. The night was reasonably clear apart from a few 'regulation' clouds at 9,000 feet. 'We might be able to use them if a Mosquito gets on our tail,' said Mahle.

The air seemed empty. In the distance we saw the ribbon of the Main. The moon treacherously lit up the great river. Then the storm broke. We were approaching the bombers. Before we had got to the enemy, the master of ceremonies had dropped his marker flares over the city. Parachute flares drifted slowly down making the night look ghostly. 'Courier 800 yards ahead,' reported Grasshof. At that moment a slight ticking began in my head-phones. Long-range nightfighters! Despite this warning I remained on course and gave my Me full throttle. The ticking grew louder. 'Mosquitos,' shouted Mahle. I took avoiding action. The British pilot's tracers went wide below my right wing. The hunt started again. Now we were flying directly over the city among the bomber stream.

Then the appalling destruction began. On the orders of the master of ceremonies four-engined bomber crews opened their bays and rained incendiaries on to the city below. The phosphorous ignited as soon as it hit the air and joined into a huge burning cloud which slowly settled on the city. It was a Dantesque and terrible sight. This fiery cloud knew no pity. It sank on churches and houses, palaces and citadels, broad avenues and narrow streets.

Then the burning veil enveloped Würzburg. In a few moments a gigantic patch of flame lit up the dark night and turned the clouds to scarlet. Würzburg was burning. By the glow of the doomed city the bombers found their direction. The small wings and slender bodies gleamed brightly. I could have shot time and time again, but as soon as I was in position, Mahle shouted: 'ACHTUNG, Mosquito!' I had instructed him only to warn me in case of great danger. Thus I dared not reflect when his words rang out. The delay of a second and we should fall like a blazing torch out of the sky. Then a four-engined Lancaster crossed my path. Without a thought I poured a long burst into its fuselage and wings. The crate exploded in the air and spun down with its crew. That was my only kill over Würzburg and incidentally my last kill of the war. It attracted the entire enemy nightfighter pack on my heels. We could hardly watch the bomber crash on the gound before they set upon us. The *Naxos* apparatus lit up constantly. Mahle no longer shouted 'Achtung' but sat and fired his tracers at the Mosquitos. No avoiding action—no banking—no hide and seek in the clouds was of any avail. The British pilot remained on my tail. Fortunately he always began from long range and his aim was inaccurate. And then suddenly Mahle shouted in terror, 'Mosquito close behind us'. His voice made me shudder. Even as I banked the burst hit my machine. There was a reek of smoke and fire. Terrifying seconds ahead, but I let my machine dive to be rid of my pursuer. We hedge-hopped over Swabia towards our airfield, Leipheim. Mahle lit up the cockpit with his torch. Everything was in order. Then he focussed it on the engine. There was a white trickle on the starboard wing. Petrol! The needle on the fuel indicator slowly sank to empty. This was a fatal situation. But misfortunes never come singly. Mahle reported reactions in the *Naxos* and the sinister tick-ticking started again in my head-phones. The British never give up. This one pursued us even to our airfield. We had to land and avoiding action was impossible. Grasshof called the airfield which replied faintly. I pumped petrol from the port to the starboard tank with the electric pump. I now spoke to the ground station myself. Everything depended on skilful landing or the Mosquito would shoot me down as I approached the runway.

'Lobster from Thrush 1. Come in please'. 'Thrush 1 from Lobster. Victor, Victor. Loud and clear. Take care—nightfighters circling the airfield.' That was to have been expected. The Britisher did not want to miss me. I replied, 'Victor, Victor. I must land. Little fuel left. I'll land blind. Put a white lamp on the landing cross and one red lamp at the end of the flarepath. Don't switch on.' The ground station had understood my plan to fool the Mosquito. Mahle sat at his guns in the rear cockpit. I lowered the wing flaps to 20 degrees and circled at low speed over the airfield. The British were searching. The ticking in my head-phones was continuous. Tensely I watched proceedings on the airfield. The perspiration was pouring from my forehead. I must rely entirely on instruments, for the two petrol lamps would neither give me my height nor the direction of the machine. Should I not let them turn on the lights just as I landed? But this seemed too risky. The Mosquitos were looking with Argus eyes at this field, and if it lit up they would immediately see the machines parked and the sheds.

The red control lights of the petrol tank lit up. That meant fuel for not more than five minutes. I must land . . . 'Lobster from Thrush 1. Hurry please. Fuel for another five minutes.' Oberfeldwebel Kramer replied at once. 'Thrush 1 from Lobster. Lamps in position. You can land.' We looked for them and Mahle was the first to discover them. They gave a very faint light. Directly above the white lamp I started the stopwatch and set my machine on its course. Mahle suddenly shouted: 'There's one ahead to starboard. A bit higher.' I only caught a glimpse of exhaust pipes disappearing in the darkness. 'For

God's sake don't shout', I replied.

The seconds passed . . . undercarriage lowered . . . any moment now the white lamp would appear in the darkness . . . there it was . . . throttle back . . . float . . . the wheels touched down . . . I put on brakes . . . we'd made it. Grasshof opened the cockpit roof. 'Herr Hauptmann the Tommies are droning right overhead. Something's up.' I cautiously gave a little throttle to prevent flames darting from the engine. Any reflection would betray us. We taxied in darkness to our dispersal pen. Then the accident happened. An over-eager mechanic, trying to be helpful, flashed his green torch. The Mosquitos were on the watch.

I turned the machine into the wind and cut off the engine. Mahle shouted, 'Put that torch out, you bloody fool.' At that moment we heard an increasingly loud whistle in the air. The Tommy was diving on the airfield. 'Quick, get out of the machine. It's going to get hot here.' Too late. The British pilot shot and the tracers made directly for us. Instinctively I ducked and there was a sinister rattle in the machine. I sprang out of my seat on to the left wing and fell over Grasshof and Mahle as I slipped to the ground. A Feldwebel was writhing on the ground. Then the second Mosquito made its attack. The burning machine made an easy target. The second burst was a winner. Our good Me 110 exploded and went up in flames. Now the British were in their element. Powerless, we had to watch two more nightfighters go up in flames. The Tommies then flew off to the west.

Feeling quite exhausted, I got on the line to Division and gave my report: 'Raid on Würzburg. British dropping phosphorous canisters. The city is on fire. Strong fighter defence. A four-engined Lancaster shot down. Machine shot up on landing by Mosquito. One dead, one wounded, two further machines destroyed.'

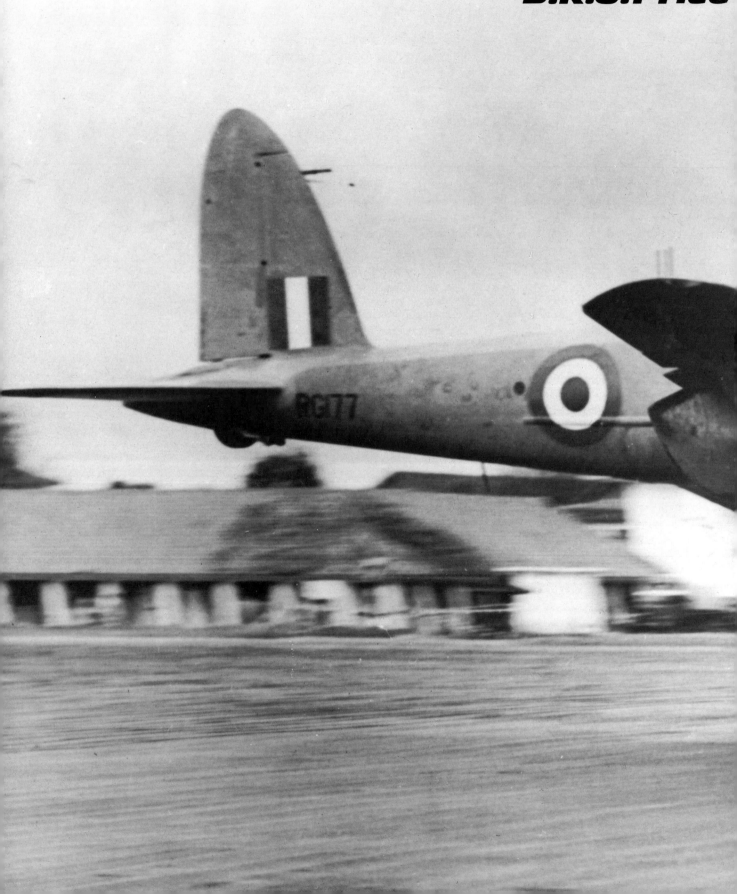

Free Lance
D.R.O. Price

Squadron line-up. 264
Squadron's crews at
Predannack on May 8, 1943.
First equipped with Mosquito
IIs in May 1942, 264 stayed
as a Mossie unit throughout
the rest of the war, claiming
its 100th 'kill' of the war on
June 10th, 1944.

Right: Squadron Leader Michael Constable-Maxwell (on wing) and his navigator, Flight Lieutenant John Quinton of 264 Squadron, at Colerne. On August 13th, 1951, Quinton selflessly gave his parachute to an Air Training Corps cadet passenger when the 228 OCU Wellington they were in had a mid-air collision. He died in the subsequent crash and today his heroism is perpetuated in the ATC's Quinton Trophy.

Below: Burma crew. Flight Sergeant J. Shortis (navigator) and Flight Lieutenant A. Torrance check for a clear take-off.

Bottom: Top-scorers—Wing Commander J. D. R. 'Bob' Braham (right) and his companion Flight Lieutenant 'Sticks' Gregory. Braham finished the war with a credited total of 29 victories, nine of these on Mosquitos.

On September 17th, 1944, a Mosquito of 29 Squadron took off from Hunsdon at 2015 hours on a free-lance patrol covering the airborne landings on a line running north to south-east of Arnhem. The crew were Lt (A) D. R. O. Price, RNVR (pilot) and Sub-Lt (A) R. E. Armitage RNVR. Crossing out from the English coast at Orfordness at 2037hrs, they made landfall on the Dutch coast at Westhoofd at 2101hrs and arrived on the patrol line at 2139hrs after some difficulty in pinpointing positions en route due to bad visibility and enemy defences. Commencing their patrol at 6,000 feet, their first radar contact came at 2205hrs. The pilot's report continued:

I was flying at 4,500 feet when my navigator obtained a contact at 2 o'clock 10°, range 4 miles, crossing starboard to port, position 25 miles from Arnhem on bearing

with oil and as the EA's speed had fallen off considerably, I broke away hard starboard and noticed that the engine had fallen out of the starboard wing of the EA which dived vertically to the deck with its port engine enveloped in flames. From 11,000 feet I was unable to follow it down owing to the steepness of the dive. The EA disappeared through low cloud and thick ground mist. I then orbited at 4,000 feet unable to see the deck and as we were not quite sure of our position, which was later estimated to be 15 miles SSW of Munster, I climbed to 6,000 feet and returned to our patrol area. As we were now overdue on patrol, I set course for home in thick cloud at 2249 hours. Crossed out Dutch coast at Westhoofd 2310 hours. In English coast at Orfordness at 2338 hours and landed base at 2355 hours. I claim one Me 110 destroyed.

Left: Fighter/Bomber crew. Flight Lieutenant W. J. Bodington, a Londoner, and Flight Sergeant B. T. Wicks from Chippingham, prior to a daylight sortie, January 1944.

Below: Night Fighters. An 85 Squadron group of high-scoring pilots. Sqn Ldr W. P. Green (26 victories), Wg Cdr John Cunningham (20) and Sqn Ldr E. D. Crew (15, plus 31 V-1s).

Bottom: Bomber Crew. Flying Officers Christensen and Dixon of 105 Squadron, 1942.

075°. I turned hard to port and contact was held at 12 o'clock, 10°, at 4 miles range. I immediately started to climb hard and followed aircraft which was taking gentle evasive action in height and azimuth. I closed range to 1,800 feet, my height being 11,000 feet, and obtained a visual on a very bright single exhaust well above and to starboard. I closed range to 1,000 feet and obtained a silhouette which was identified as an Me 110 carrying long-range tanks slung under the wings, outboard of each engine, at 300 feet range. My navigator also confirmed identification.

Just before the visual was obtained, the EA started to make hard port and starboard turns also throttling hard back, causing the engines to emit vast showers of sparks. In spite of this evasive action, contact was held and range was opened to 150 yards. 'Waggle your wings or you will burn' was given without response from the EA which also gave no response to IFF interrogation. I fired a 3-second burst on a very bright white exhaust on the starboard engine causing it to explode with debris flying off. The windscreen was covered

Combat Report
Russ Bannock

Aussie Team. Sergeant T. N.
Gibbons and Les Brodie of
464 Squadron, Hunsdon,
1944.

Right: Fighter Leader. Wing Commander Desmond Hughes, DSO DFC, Commanding Officer, 604 Squadron, 1944 who ended the war credited with 18 air victories.

Far right: Squadron Commander. John Wooldridge, who succeeded to the command of 105 Squadron on March 17th, 1943 and led many of the unit's highly successful raids against German targets.

Bottom right: Tribute from the Erks. Wing Commander Roy Ralston, DSO, AFC, DFM accepting a model of his Mosquito from the ground crews of 105 Squadron, April 1943, when Roy was posted to a 'mahogany bomber' tour at PFF Headquarters.

Bomber Leader. Wing Commander Hughie Edwards VC DSO DFC, one-time commander of the first Mosquito squadron, 105, 1942.

'Russ' Bannock with his regular observer, R. Bruce, were a particularly successful Mosquito fighter crew and by the end of the war were credited with nine enemy aircraft destroyed, plus 19 V1 guided missiles. Typical of their sorties was this one on September 12th, 1944 when they took off from Hunsdon airfield on a *Flower* sortie in support of Bomber Command. They were then serving with 418 Squadron RCAF and in the following month Bannock was appointed Commanding Officer of the unit.

We crossed the French coast at Coxyde at 2254 hours and proceeded directly to the target area (Illesheim). After patrolling in the target area from 0044 hours to 0212 hours, we set course homeward. While passing just south of Kitzsingen at 0220 hours we saw this aerodrome lit with double flare-path and east/west V/L. The right-hand bar of the outer and inner horizons were not lit. We commenced to prowl around the airfield at about 400 feet and almost immediately observed an **aircraft** with navigation lights on coming **towards** us, doing a steep climbing turn towards the aerodrome. I did a 180° turn to port and followed the aircraft which was climbing very steeply over the airfield. I positioned myself at about 125 yards behind and slightly below and fired a 1½ second burst of **cannon** and machine gun at about 5° angle-off to starboard. There were numerous strikes on the starboard side of the fuselage and along the starboard wing. Almost immediately I fired another 1½-second burst of both cannon and machine gun fire from the same position. Numerous strikes were again observed along the starboard wing and fuselage and the starboard engine exploded. The aircraft immediately dropped straight down and as we passed over it I started a turn to the right to observe the results. During the turn there was a large flash on the ground below us, but as we completed the turn we would not see any fire on the ground. Since there was not a fire, we are claiming this aircraft as only probably destroyed, but as the starboard engine was seen to explode, and the subsequent flash seen from an explosion on the ground, we are almost certain that it crashed and request that the claim be raised to destroyed.

In Foreign Climes

Left: The first Mosquito to arrive in Malta, DZ230, (A-Able), a Mk II intruder of 23 Squadron, which reached the beleaguered island on December 27th, 1942, touching down at Luqa airstrip in the capable hands of Wing Commander Peter Wykeham-Barnes.

Below left: NFXII, HK128, ('JT-G') of 256 Squadron at Luqa, 1944. The small aerial aft of the main radio aerial was part of the 'Identification, friend or foe' (IFF) equipment. The officer is Flying officer L. Southern, signals Officer of 256 Squadron. A detachment of six of 256's Mossies first arrived in Malta on July 2nd, 1943, to be joined by the rest of the squadron in October.

Bottom left: Mileage Mossie. NS688, a PRXVI of Transport Command, setting out to fly to Karachi, India, November 1944. The trip was accomplished in a total flying time of 14 hours and 37 minutes.

Right: Jungle Strip—a navigator's view of the landing strip at Agartala on February 4th, 1944, the base for 27 Squadron. 27 was the first squadron in India/Burma to receive Mosquitos, for tropical trials; the first aircraft DZ695, a MkII, arriving on April 11th, 1943. Eventually, 27 formed one flight for operations but soon exchanged them for the unit's main equipment, Beaufighters.

Below: 'O.K. Starboard'. A PRXVI Mosquito starts up on a Bengal airfield with LAC J. S. Gillam providing the help.

Bottom right: An FBVI negotiates the aftermath of a monsoon rainstorm in Burma.

Above: Photo-reconnaissance PRXVIs undergoing major inspections in India. The nearest carried an overall blue doping, while MM367 in the background was finished in a silver dope.

Below: From November 9th, 1945, although the war was over, 84 and 110 Squadrons were called on to operate during the initial teething troubles surrounding the birth of the new Indonesian nation. Strike and reconnaissance sorties continued until March 1946. Here, 84 Squadron's FBVIs are seen lined up at Kemajoran, Malaya in 1946.

Right: 84 Squadron, Seletar, Singapore in 1946.

Far middle right: Mosquito Graveyard—remnants of various Far East Mossies dumped or collected together at Seletar, December 1946. HR526 (PY-B) was ex-84 Squadron, while several ex-PR aircraft are evident.

Far bottom right: The last op—Mosquito PR34, RG314 of 81 Squadron, Seletar, making the final Mosquito sortie in RAF service on December 15th, 1955.

Paint and Pride

Above: Top Dog—LR503, (F) of 105 Squadron which ended the war with a Bomber Command record of 213 operational sorties in the fighter/bomber role. In this view the 203rd completed op is proudly recorded in white dope, watched by the crew who flew it.

Right: '203—and still going strong'.

Left: LR503 with its full record inscribed. The crew pictured here are (right) Flight Lieutenant Maurice Briggs, DSO DFC DFM and his navigator, Flying Officer John Baker DFC (Bar) who flew the veteran Mosquito to Canada at the end of the European war for demonstration, but on May 10th, 1945, during a flying display at Calgary Airport, LR503 suddenly plunged into the ground, killing Briggs and Baker.

Top: 'D-Dorothy', ML897, a
PR Mk IX which totted up a
total of 161 sorties in advance
of Bomber Command and
8th USAAF raids over
Germany, serving with 1409
Bomber Command
Meteorological Flight,
Wyton. In its career, D flew
as bomber, marker, high and
low reconnaissance and met.
recce.

Above: D-Dorothy landing at
Wyton after its 153rd sortie
in November 1944.

Right: LAC Bennett painting
up Dorothy's 141st completed
operation on the 'log'—each
marked by a small lightning
flash.

Right: The Joker of 105 Squadron, June 1943—usually referred to on the unit as the Gremlin King.

Far right: 'Moonshine McSwine'—displaying 15 victory-symbol swastikas on its 'sharp end'. In front, two of the several successful 418 squadron intruder crews; Sqn Ldr H. D. Cleveland and his navigator, F/Sgt F. Day, Lt J. E. Luma DFC (USAAF) and navigator, Fg Off C. G. Finlayson RCAF. Between them they claimed 22 air and ground 'kills'.

Top left: *Oboe* Pathfinder—BIV, DK331, ('D') of 109 Squadron at RAF Wyton, August 1943, displaying a bomb log of 40 completed ops and an ornate winged dragon insignia on its nose. Personnel from left are Squadron Leader E. L. Ifould (nav), Wing Commander Hal Bufton, Corporal Wright and two un-named ground crew.

Top middle left: 'Grim Reaper'—another 109 Squadron *Oboe* pioneer, DK333, ('F'), bearing a bomb log of 29 ops and the grisly character from which the Mossie received its nickname.

Left: In lighter vein, Wing Commander John de L. Wooldridge, DSO DFC DFM, alongside his 105 Squadron aircraft, 'Knave of Diamonds' on June 28th, 1943.

Far middle left: Squadron Leader Bill Blessing, DSO DFC, 'A' Flight Commander in 105 Squadron with his 'Knave of Spades', June 1943. Blessing was lost in action over Caen on July 7th, 1944 during a PFF marking sortie.

Centre: A swan with teeth. Night intruder with shark-mouth markings which destroyed three enemy aircraft; two of them in addition to four trains in a single night's work. Flying Officer P. D. Wood, 605 Squadron, left was awarded a DFC for his part in the feat.

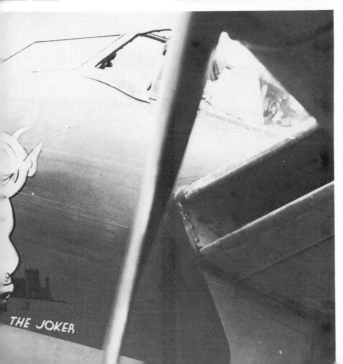

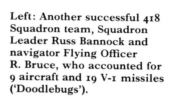

Left: Another successful 418 Squadron team, Squadron Leader Russ Bannock and navigator Flying Officer R. Bruce, who accounted for 9 aircraft and 19 V-1 missiles ('Doodlebugs').

Right: Invasion stripes—applying the black and white mandatory markings for all Allied aircraft on June 4th, 1944, two days before the Normandy invasion.

Left: The swastika-marked Mosquito of Flight Lieutenant Blomley DFC and his navigator; 605 Squadron, Castle Camps airfield, June 1943.

Far left: A fanciful Popeye punching a Japanese 'serpent' figured on the hatch door of Flight Lieutenant A. Torrance's Burma Mosquito.

Right: 'Wolf'—the aircraft of Squadron Leader Heath DFC (BAR); 605 Squadron, Castle Camps, June 1943.

Below left: VIP marking. Mosquito BIX, bearing the official rank pennant and 'stars' of Air Marshal Sir Arthur Coningham, KCB, DSO, MC, AFC, who at that time (August 1944) was AOC-in-C, 2nd Tactical Air Force in Germany.

Below: Civil Livery. HJ720, a converted Mk VI, registered as G-AGGF, taxying out at Leuchars on Imperial Airways service prior to a flight to Stockholm, early 1943. It was lost on August 17th, 1943 when it crashed at Invermairk, Glen Esk, killing its crew, Captain L. A. Wilkins and Radio Officer N. H. Beaumont.

Target Amiens

The many examples of the Mosquitos' ability to bomb a pinpoint target included such classic examples as Shell House, Copenhagen, Aarhus, Oslo, Egletons and dozens more. All were outstandingly successful operations, utterly destroying individual buildings containing Gestapo archives or similar unique objectives. Probably the most poignant operation was the now-legendary attack on Amiens. Its purpose was literally to save lives—nearly 700 courageous French Resistance workers, many of whom were on the eve of execution for their part in helping the Allied cause. The mission was specific—to initiate a break-out from Amiens gaol, at that time a collecting point for condemned French patriots due to be executed by the Gestapo. This was to be accomplished by crumbling the outer walls and demolishing certain internal buildings containing German guards. Absolute precision bombing was vital. Just a few inches or seconds miscalculation by

After postponements because of impossible weather conditions, the Mosquito crews of 140 Wing were called for early briefing on the morning of February 18th 1944. Three formations of six aircraft, each crewed by the most experienced pilots and navigators of 487, 464 and 21 Squadrons were detailed for the operation. Another Mosquito from the Film Production Unit would follow to photograph results. The first wave was to comprise two Vics of three Mosquitos from the New Zealand unit, 487 Squadron; followed by two Vics of the Australian 464 Squadron. 21 Squadron's Mosquitos were to be held in reserve read to complete any unfinished part of the job. Master-minding the operation in the air was a tall, blond Group Captain with four years of almost continuous operational experience behind him, Percy Charles Pickard, DSO DFC. Responsible for the whole navigation plot was Pickard's inseparable friend and navigator, Flight Lieutenant J. A. 'Bill' Broadley, DSO DFC DFM. It was to be their last operation together, for both found death and immortality at Amiens. The photo Mosquito, DZ414, 'O-Orange' piloted by Tony Wickham, was to follow

Above: Group Captain Percy Charles Pickard, DSO DFC— leader of the legendary gaol-busting mission against Amiens prison.

Top right: Pickard's friend Flight Lieutenant J. A. 'Bill' Broadley, DSO DFC DFM who master-navigated the Amiens operation.

Middle right: Minutes to go. Bill Broadley makes a final adjustment to Pickard's microphone leads just before take-off on February 18th, 1944 at Hunsdon. In the background is Mosquito HX922 (EG-F) in which both men flew the mission and in which they died.

Right: Tight trio of 487 Squadron's Mosquitos.

the Mosquito crews would mean a difference between possible freedom or wholesale death for the French inmates.

The mission was originally requested by the French Maquis, a desperate final attempt to rescue their countrymen. Although the RAF had qualms about such an attack with its inevitable possibility of killing the very people they were asked to save, no one could, or wanted to refuse to at least try. It meant placing bombs almost as if by hand in particular sections of the prison structure to facilitate the final escape. It meant low-level bombing runs at no more than 15 feet, pinpoint bombing and then an immediate steep climb to avoid the 60 feet-high structure of the prison buildings. It meant precision timing between aircraft on the run-in. And it could be done only once. Yet when the crews of 140 Wing, 2 Group, RAF were told the object of the mission at briefing, every man wanted to take part. As one pilot described it, 'There was no mistaking the air of determination.'

in after the second wave's attack, while Pickard would circuit the area and decide if the third wave was needed. Fighter escorts, 12 Typhoons from 198 Squadron, would take care of any Luftwaffe interference. Each Mosquito was to be loaded with two 500lb bombs, fused with 11-second delay detonators. The New Zealanders were to breach the outer wall of the prison in two places, while the Australians were to rupture the main prison building inside by destroying the German guards' annex at the base of the main structure. Only three minutes maximum were allowed between these two attacks.

For two hours the crews studied a replica model of the prison, calculating angles, heights, obstacles, gun-posts, run-out routes. Then, dispersing to their aircraft, by 1030 hours all 19 Mosquitos were parked at the turn-round of Hunsdon's main runway, ready for an 1100-hours take-off. The raid was scheduled to commence over the gaol at precisely 1203 hours, when the first Vic of New Zealanders would make their drop. Flying Officer N. M. Sparks, one of those first three captains, takes up the story.

We were determined to give everything we could to this job. I remember Group Captain Pickard putting into words what we were all beginning to feel when he said, 'Well, boys, this is a death-or-glory show. If it succeeds it will be one of the most worth-while ops of the war. If you never do anything else you can still count this as the finest job you could ever have done.' So we went outside and looked at the weather again. It was terrible! Snow was still falling, sweeping in gusts that every now and then hid the end of the runway from sight. If this had been an ordinary operation we were doing it would pretty certainly have been scrubbed—put off to another day. But this was not an ordinary job; every day, perhaps every hour, might be the last in the lives of those Frenchmen. We got into our aircraft warmed up the engines, and sat there thinking it was no kind of weather to go flying in, but somehow knowing that we must. And when we saw the Group Captain drive up in his car, and get out of it and into his own Mosquito, we knew for certain that the show was on. The 18 aircraft took off quickly, one after another, at about 11 in the morning—we were going to hit the prison when the guards were at lunch. By the time I got to 100 feet I could not see a thing except that grey soupy mist

and snow and rain beating against the perspex window. There was no hope of either getting into formation or staying in it, and I headed straight for the Channel coast. Two miles out from the coast the weather was beautifully clear, and it was only a matter of minutes before we were over France. We skimmed across the coast at deck level, swept round the north of Amiens and then split up for the attack.

My own aircraft, with our Wing Commander's and one other, stayed together to make the first run-in; our job was to blast a hole in the eastern wall. We picked up the straight road that runs from Albert to Amiens, and that led us straight to the prison. I shall never forget that road—long and straight and covered with snow. It was lined with tall poplars and the three of us were flying so low that I had to keep my aircraft tilted at an angle to avoid hitting the tops of the trees with my wing. It was then, as I flew with one eye on those poplars and the other watching the road ahead that I was reminded we had a fighter escort. A Typhoon came belting across right in front of us and I nearly jumped out of my seat. The poplars suddenly petered out and there, a mile ahead, was the prison. It looked just like the briefing model and we were almost on top of it within a few seconds. We hugged

the ground as low as we could, and at the lowest possible speed; we pitched our bombs towards the base of the wall, fairly scraped over it—and our part of the job was over. There was not time to stay and watch the results. We had to get straight out and let the others come in; and when we turned away we could see the second New Zealand section make their attack and follow out behind us.

Wing Commander I. S. 'Black' Smith, DFC, leading that first Vic of Mosquitos commented afterwards, 'My section went right in for the corner of the east walls, while the others drew off a few miles and made their run-in on the north wall. Navigation was perfect and I've never done a better flight. It was like a Hendon demonstration. We flew as low and as slowly as possible, aiming to drop our bombs right at the foot of the wall. Even so, our bombs went across the first wall and across the courtyard, exploding on the wall at the other side. I dropped my own bombs from a height of 10 feet, pulling hard on the stick. The air was thick with smoke but of all the bombs dropped by both my section and the other, only one went astray.'

As soon as the New Zealanders had cleared the target, 464 Squadron, led by

Four stages of the actual bombing of Amiens prison. Left: Breaking away over the Albert-Amiens road which ran alongside the prison after bomb release. Bottom left: Inner buildings just after bomb impact. Centre: Stoked up—the German guard billets burning. Below: A reconnaissance photo shortly after the raid, showing the damage achieved, particularly the break in the outer wall of the courtyard.

Wing Commander R. W. 'Bob' Iredale, DFC, swept in to complete the second bombing phase—demolition of the German guards' annex. Flying so low that they had to lift over the outer walls and immediately skid their bombs in, the Australians flew straight through thick smoke and debris thrown up by the preceding New Zealanders' exploding bombs.

Meanwhile, circling the objective, Pickard saw that the job had been successfully accomplished. Gaping holes in the outer walls were disgorging escaping prisoners, tiny black ant-like figures starkly contrasted against the whiteness of the snow landscape, and accordingly he gave the order for the reserve squadron to return to base—their bombs were not needed. Tony Wickham in the photo Mosquito started his first run over the prison. 'We could see, the first time we flew over the objective, that the operation had been a complete success. Both ends of the prison had been completely demolished, and the surrounding wall broken down in many places. We could see a large number of prisoners escaping along the road. The cameras fixed in the plane were steadily recording it all, and the photographer was crouched in the nose taking picture after picture, as fast as he could. He was so enthusiastic that he got us to stay over the objective longer than I considered healthy. After each run I would suggest to him that we about-turned and made for England, and he would answer, "Oh! no . . . do it again. Just once more". But eventually he was satisfied and we headed for home.'

Smoothly as the whole operation had gone, it was not without loss. Squadron Leader I. R. McRitchie, leader of the second Australian wave, was re-forming near Albert when flak riddled his Mosquito, MM404, killing his navigator, Flight Lieutenant R. W. Sampson, and seriously wound McRitchie. With instinctive superlative skill, the pilot crash-landed at over 200mph and survived to become a prisoner of war. It was almost certainly McRitchie's crash which attracted the attention of the mission leader, Percy Pickard, who was seen to fly low over the spot, presumably checking for survivors. Within seconds two Focke-Wulf 190s had fastened on the tail

of his Mosquito, HX922, 'F-Freddie', one opened fire and the Mosquito flicked over on to its back and ploughed straight into the ground. Neither Pickard nor Broadley survived. Three other Mosquitos were seriously damaged but returned to England. But the object of the raid had been admirably achieved. Of the 700 or more prisoners in Amiens jail 258 escaped, including at least 12 who were due to be shot the next day. Others were recaptured or killed during the action (some of these by the German guards). About 50 German staff were killed during the bombing.

Today, the actual model used for briefing 140 Wing's crews, along with a door lock from one of the prison cells from which one prisoner escaped successfully, can be seen in the galleries of the Imperial War Museum, London. And in Amiens is a memorial, erected in 1945 to the memory of Percy Pickard and Bill Broadley, leaders of one of the war's most brilliant Mosquito operations.

One crew which did not return. Squadron Leader A. I. McRitchie, DFC (left) and his navigator, Flight Lieutenant R. W. Sampson, of 464 Squadron, RAAF, 140 Wing who, in MM404, (SB-T) were shot down by flak near Amiens; Sampson being killed outright and McRitchie being wounded. The latter crashlanded at well over 200mph, yet survived to become a prisoner of war.

Left: Close-up of the break in one of the inner walls.

Right: Spy in the Sky. VL618, representative of the vital PRU Mosquitos, Mk PR 34. No 1 PRU at Benson was, in fact, the first RAF unit to receive Mosquitos, W4051 (its initial example) arriving at Benson on July 13th, 1941. The first PRU operations with Mossies took place on September 17th, 1941—a recce of Brest harbour and the Spanish-French border. In the Burma campaign, PR Mosquitos played an unpublicised, but supremely important role in the air campaigns.

Far right: The Oxford Dictionary defines 'Mosquito' as 'Gnat-like insect, some biting severely . . .'. Perhaps the major version used to bite the enemy was the fighter bomber version, the FBVI, exemplified here by NS893 on its pre-delivery test flight. Fighter and fighter/bomber varieties equipped a total of 55 Squadrons of the RAF.

Far left: Daddy of the Bombers. W4072 ,the prototype for the BIV line of Mosquito raiders, which first flew on September 8th, 1941, shown here with two 1250hp Rolls Royce Merlin XXI Series 1 powerplants. As D-Dog of 105 Squadron, it flew the first Mosquito bombing raid; taking 2 x 250lb and 2 x 500lb HE bombs to Cologne at dawn on May 31st, 1942.

Left: Black Beastie. DD750, an NF Mk II in the contemporary 1942 soot-black finish. The first night fighter squadron of Mossies was 157, formed at Debden on December 13th, 1941. Receiving its first aircraft on January 26th, 1942; 157's first operations were flown on the night of April 27th.

Far middle left: In contrast to the previous photo, MM748, an NF Mk 30, represents the tremendous advances made in nightfighting apparatus within the short space of two years. Mk 30s were first flown in March 1944, being basically a development of the NFXIX with two-step Merlin 72 or 76 engines and AI MkX. By 1945 a total of 17 units had been part- or fully equipped with Mk 30s.

Left: Pot Belly, the MkXVI ML991 with a bulged bomb bay enabling the compact design to carry a 4,000lb HC 'cookie'. The PFF Light Night Striking Force dropped at least 1,459 'cookies' between January 1st and April 21st, 1945. In all, No. 8 Group dropped about 10,000 of these blast bombs during its offensive.

Above: Coastal Killer. With its battery of four 20mm cannons, four .303 machine guns and eight 3-inch rocket projectiles, this 143 Squadron strike Mosquito was a formidable destroyer. Among their many successes against enemy shipping, 10 U-Boats were sunk by Coastal Command Mossies.

Above: Day Bombers. A trio of Australian-crewed FBVIs of 464 Squadron in September 1944, en route to a train-busting session in East Normandy. The nearest aircraft, N-Nuts, is serialled NS843.

Left: Beat-Up. RG177, a Mosquito PR34A of 81 Squadron, Seletar, piloted by Flight Sergeant Anderson, clips the grass in May 1953.

Right: Formation Stuff. Three neat vics of 25 Squadron's Mk 36s in September 1946 as the unit arrived at its 'permanent' peace-time base at West Malling.

Above: Port Feathered—an FBVI demonstrating complete confidence in 'engine-out' performance. All else being equal, a Mosquito FBVI with full war load could maintain height on either engine up to roughly 12,000ft provided climbing power at about 150 knots was maintained. A single-engine take-off was possible providing a safety speed of at least 155 knots at plus-9lb/sq. inch boost had been reached the prop was immediately feathered and the radiator shutter closed.

Far left: Waiting to go. HK419, (B-Beer) of 96 Squadron at dispersal on West Malling airfield, 1943. 96 was particularly successful in anti-'Diver' patrols (attacking the German V-1 guided missiles) during 1944, destroying 49 in June, 1944 alone.

Above: Four-blades. MP469, the prototype pressure-cabin bomber, modified to NFXV standards, for high-altitude fighting. Armament was four .303 Browning machine guns in an under-belly detachable pack. AI Mk VIII radar was nose-installed.

Far right: Four-Blades en Masse. A row of refurbished FBVIs bought and operated by the Turkish Air Force, post-1945.

Right: The Final Indignity— PF606, originally built as a BXVI and converted to TT Mk 39 for Fleet Target Towing role. The 'green-house' nose accommodated a camera man, while the former bomb bay became the housing for an electrically-driven winch, its operator having a dorsal cupola.

Below right and far bottom right: Two photographs which virtually sum up the essential teams which between them put the Mosquito into the air.
Below right: An anonymous crew and their equally anonymous aircraft—a magnificent fighting trio and . . .
. . . Far bottom right: the 'Erks' who toiled hard, long and faithfully to 'keep 'em flying'. Tea-break on a far east Mosquito dispersal of BXVIs. The quality of the groundcrews' faithful service usually received little publicity—but without their sweat and blisters, the Mosquito story would have been very different.

In Memory Of...

Leading Aircraftman Albert Sullivan and Marie Yvonne tend the original grave of Group Captain P. C. Pickard and Flight Lieutenant J. A. Broadley, both killed during the raid on Amiens Prison.